Guitar Folksong Duets
For Pupil and Teacher
Volume 2

By Adrian Allan

Edited by Allan H. Jones

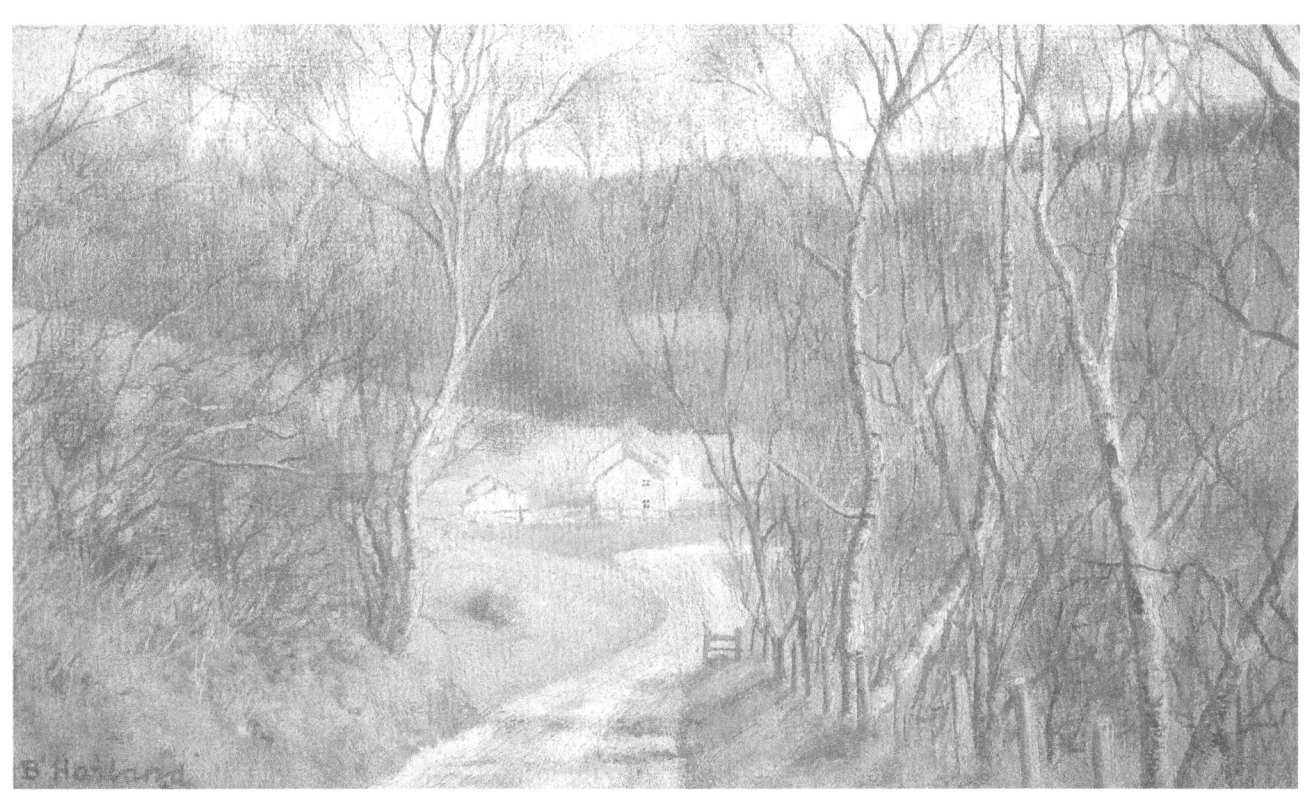

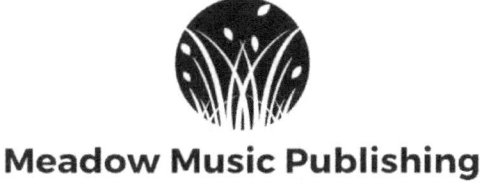

Meadow Music Publishing

First Edition: 2018

ISBN 978-0-244-98559-2

Meadow Music Publishing
23c Burford Rd
Manchester, M16 8EW

adrianallan12345@gmail.com

www.facebook.com/meadowmusicpublishing/

Front cover illustration "Staindale" by B.Harland

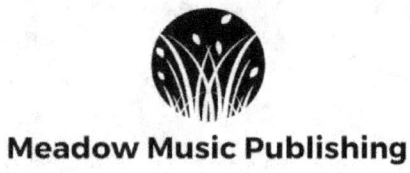

Meadow Music Publishing

Contents

Preface

After publishing the first edition of Guitar Folksong Duets for Pupil and Teacher in 2016, I decided to write a second volume. The aims are the same as the first volume; to provide a selection of tuneful early-grade melodic line pieces, accompanied by effective teacher parts. However, in this volume the range of songs is more varied and covers a wider area of Europe.

The melodies range from the very simple, such as *I Know Where I'm Going*, to pieces that require some understanding of more challenging rhythmic patterns or keys signatures with up to two sharps.

I hope that teachers and pupils will enjoy playing these pieces as much as I have enjoyed the task of researching and arranging them.

A note on the music

A Basque Lullaby. This is a haunting melody from the Basque region, in northern Spain.

Beyond the Mountains is a song from Switzerland that combines the regret of leaving home and the optimism of finding somewhere new: "There lies a world beyond the mountains, there lies a world for me to see".

Early One Morning. This well-known English song first appeared in 1787, but the melody that we know was written by William Chappell in his book, English National Airs, c. 1855-1859.

Fishermen's Evening Song. This song from Brittany was used to boost the morale of men setting forth to fish at night, "One song my comrades, 'ere we go. Listen to the glad waves call."

Geordie. A song that is thought to originate in England, but has found its way across many continents. It is narrated by a young woman who laments for a man who is to face execution for his crimes. The woman begs the judge for clemency.

Golden Fish Swimming in the Lake is a Polish song that tells of the joys of fishing, "Let us go and catch all the fish we can, whatever be the weather."

Goodnight is a touching lullaby from the Czech Republic, "Goodnight, dear, softly sleep, sweet be the dreams of your slumber deep."

I Know Where I'm Going is a simple song from Scotland that tells of a young woman's resolve to marry "handsome, winsome Johnny".

I'm Seventeen Come Sunday is a rather quirky little tune that can be traced back to the eighteenth century. It is written from the viewpoint of a young man who sees a "handsome maid just as the sun was rising".

I Would Soothe You is a lullaby, sung in Gaelic, from Uist in the Outer Hebrides.

Megan's Fair Daughter is a song about unrequited love from Wales.

O Vermeland is a poignant melody from Sweden. Anders Fryxell used the tune in his 1822 play *The girl from Vermland* and wrote the lyrics. Shortly before his death in 1881 he admitted that the melody he had used was not his but he believed it to be a folk tune.

Poor Old Horse is an English folk song that is narrated from the viewpoint of an old horse. It starts off with, "When I was young and in my prime", and ends up with, "The dogs shall eat my rotten flesh."

Robin Redbreast is a Welsh song from the region of Carnarvonshire. It tells of a robin who visits a children's home in the winter.

Santa Lucia is a traditional Neapolitan barcarolle which celebrates the waterfront district Borga Santa Lucia in the bay of Naples. It has been recorded by Elvis Presley, Bing Crosby and many others.

Shoes of Shining Leather is a Hungarian song that is often sung as a round, as the arrangement hints at here.

Shule Aroon is a song of lamentation from the eighteenth century. The verses refer to a lover's enlistment in the Irish Brigade (1691-1740).

The Life That's Free is a traditional song from Alsace, an historical region on France's eastern border with Germany.

The Lorelei tells of the exploits of a wicked maiden who lures fishermen to their death in a whirlpool in the River Rhine.

The Minstrel Boy is a traditional Irish song that describes the proud fate of a warrior bard.

The Old Home is a folk song from the Low Countries (Belgium, Netherlands and Luxembourg). It is nostalgic and tells of polders, mills and dykes that "leads to my home".

There Came A Little Stranger is an old French carol which starts with the lyrics, "There came a little stranger, Noel, Noel, Christ is born".

Where the Gentian Blows is a folk song from the Tyrol, an historical region in northern Italy and western Austria. Gentian is a blue Alpine plant. It is used to flavour a distilled beverage consumed in the Alps.

Will Ye Go, Lassie is also known as "Wild Mountain Thyme". The lyrics and melody are a variant of the song "The Braes of Balquhither" by Scottish poet Robert Tannahill (1774–1810), a contemporary of Robert Burns.

Will Ye No' Come Back Again is a poem by Carolina Oliphant (Lady Nairne) set to a traditional Scottish folk tune about Bonnie Prince Charlie, the leader of the Jacobite rebellion who fled to France after the battle of Culloden near Inverness in 1746.

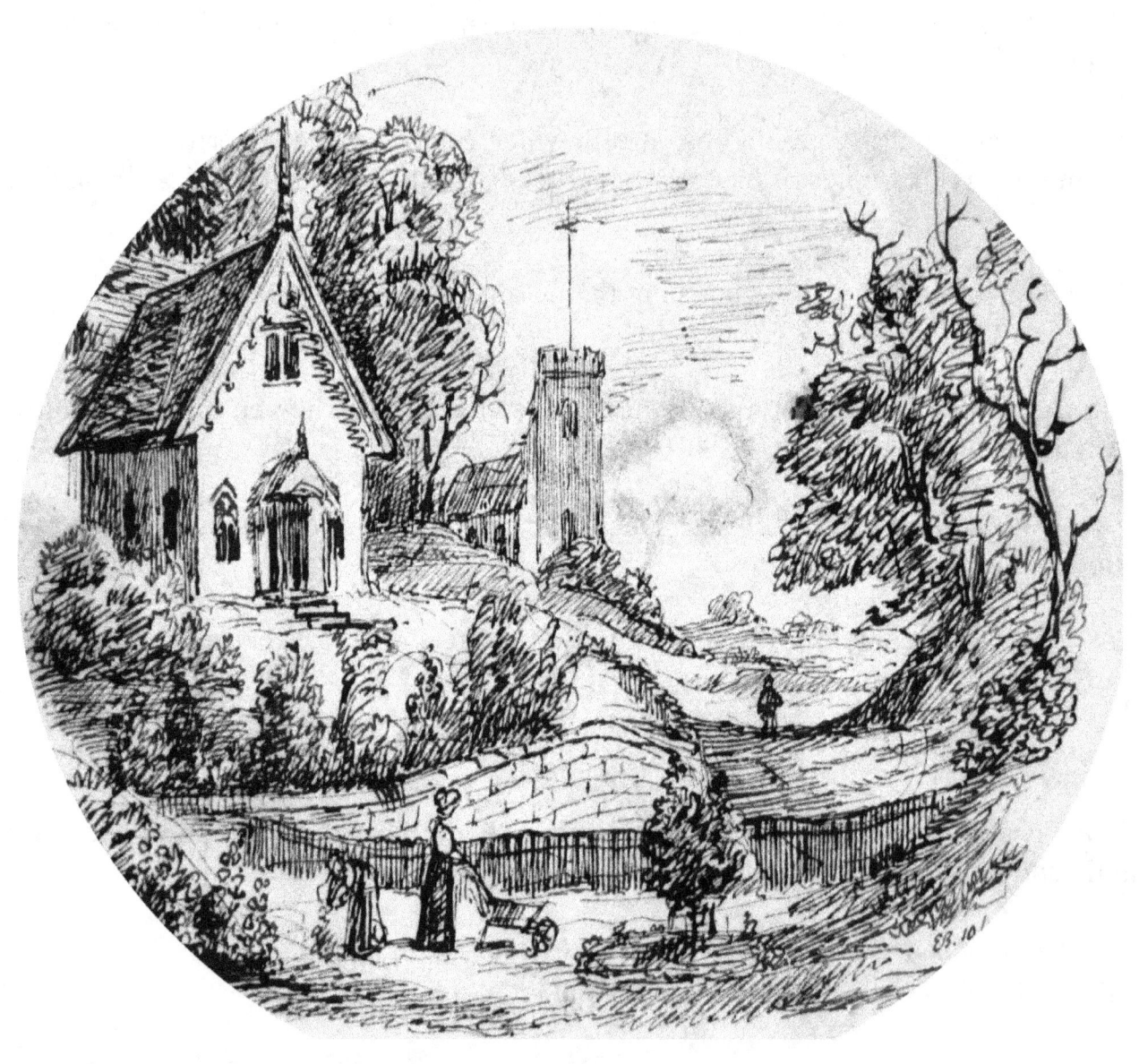

Origin of Songs in this Book

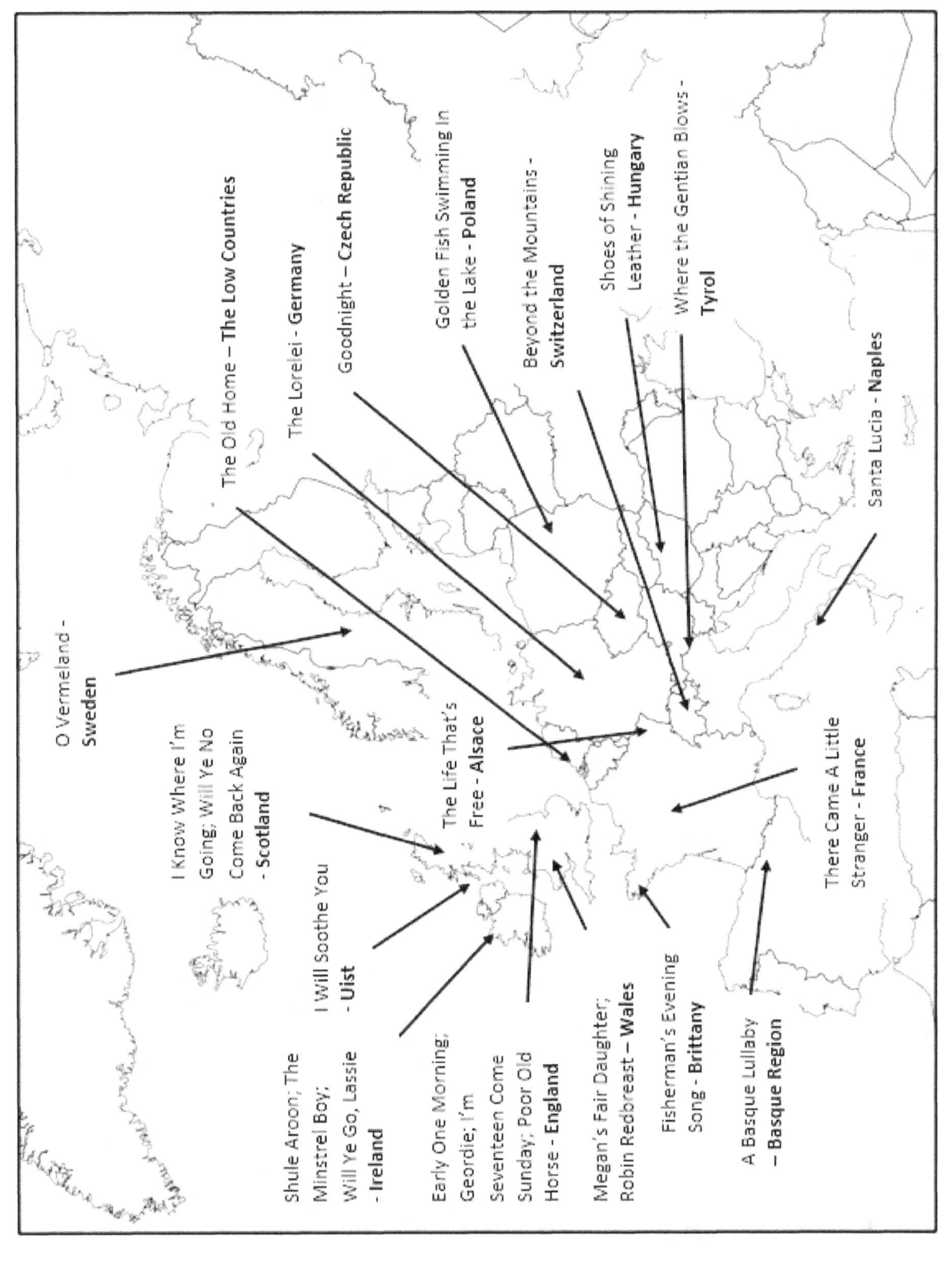

O Vermeland - Sweden

I Know Where I'm Going; Will Ye No Come Back Again - Scotland

Shule Aroon; The Minstrel Boy; Will Ye Go, Lassie - Ireland

I Will Soothe You - Uist

Early One Morning; Geordie; I'm Seventeen Come Sunday; Poor Old Horse - England

The Life That's Free - Alsace

Megan's Fair Daughter; Robin Redbreast – Wales

Fisherman's Evening Song - Brittany

A Basque Lullaby – Basque Region

The Old Home – The Low Countries

The Lorelei - Germany

Goodnight – Czech Republic

Golden Fish Swimming In the Lake - Poland

Beyond the Mountains - Switzerland

Shoes of Shining Leather - Hungary

Where the Gentian Blows - Tyrol

Santa Lucia - Naples

There Came A Little Stranger - France

A Basque Lullaby

Traditional Basque

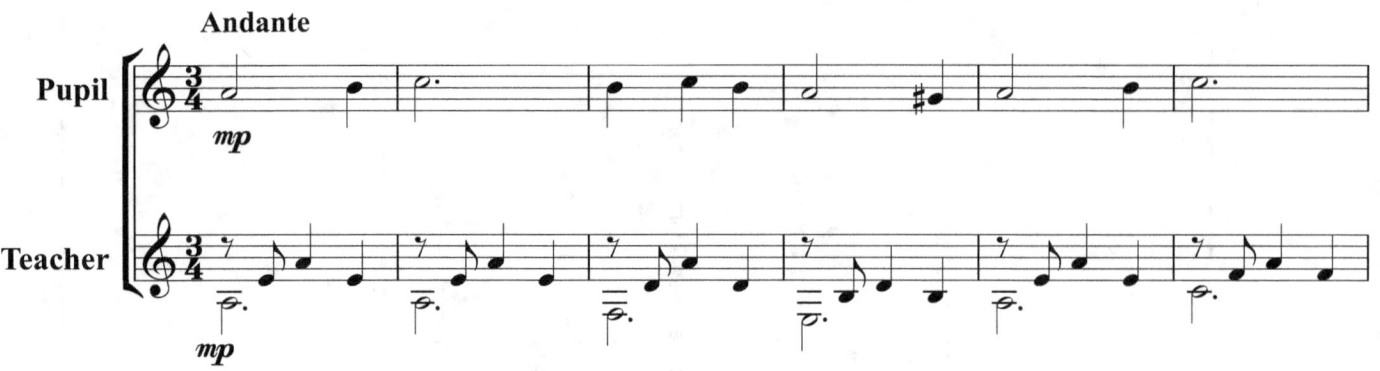

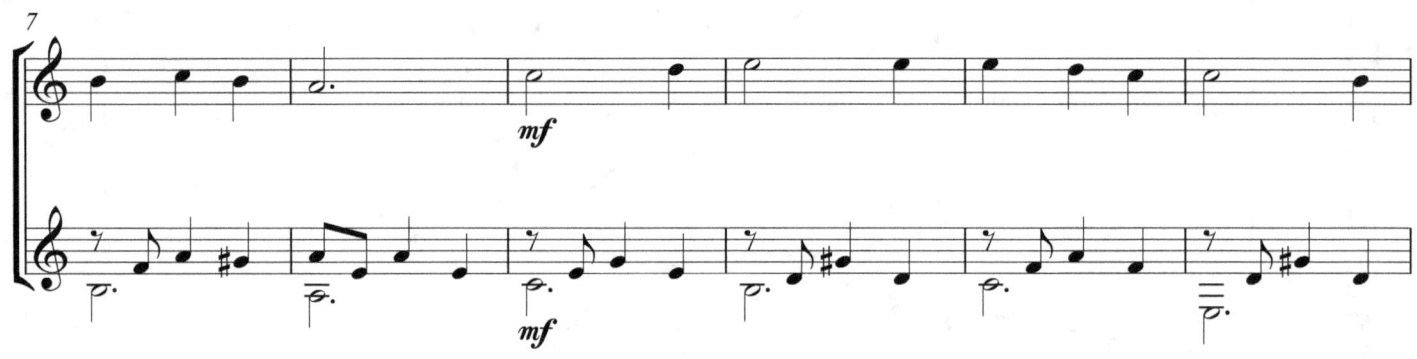

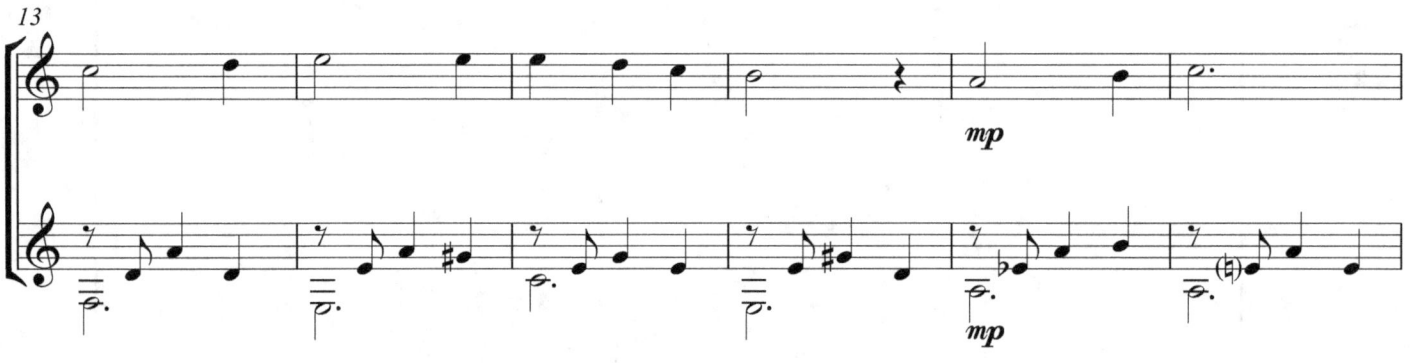

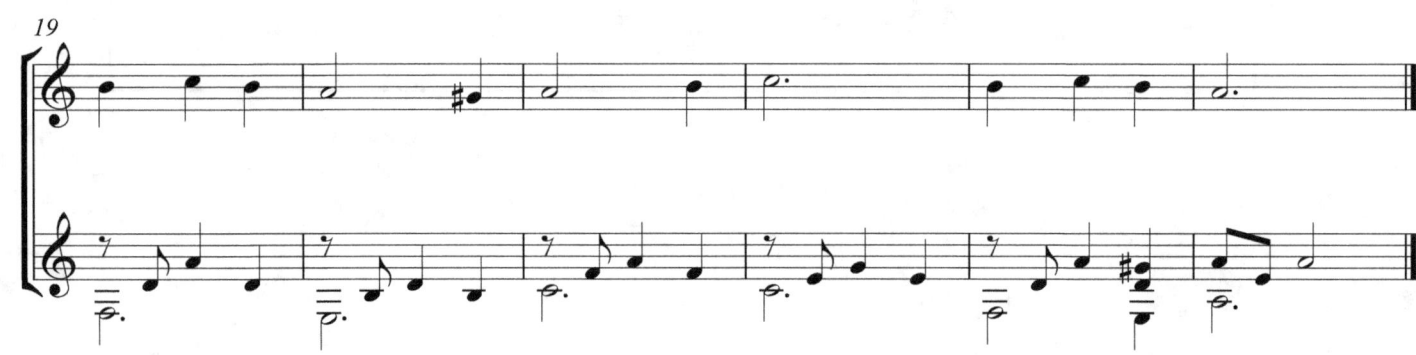

Beyond The Mountains

Traditional Swiss

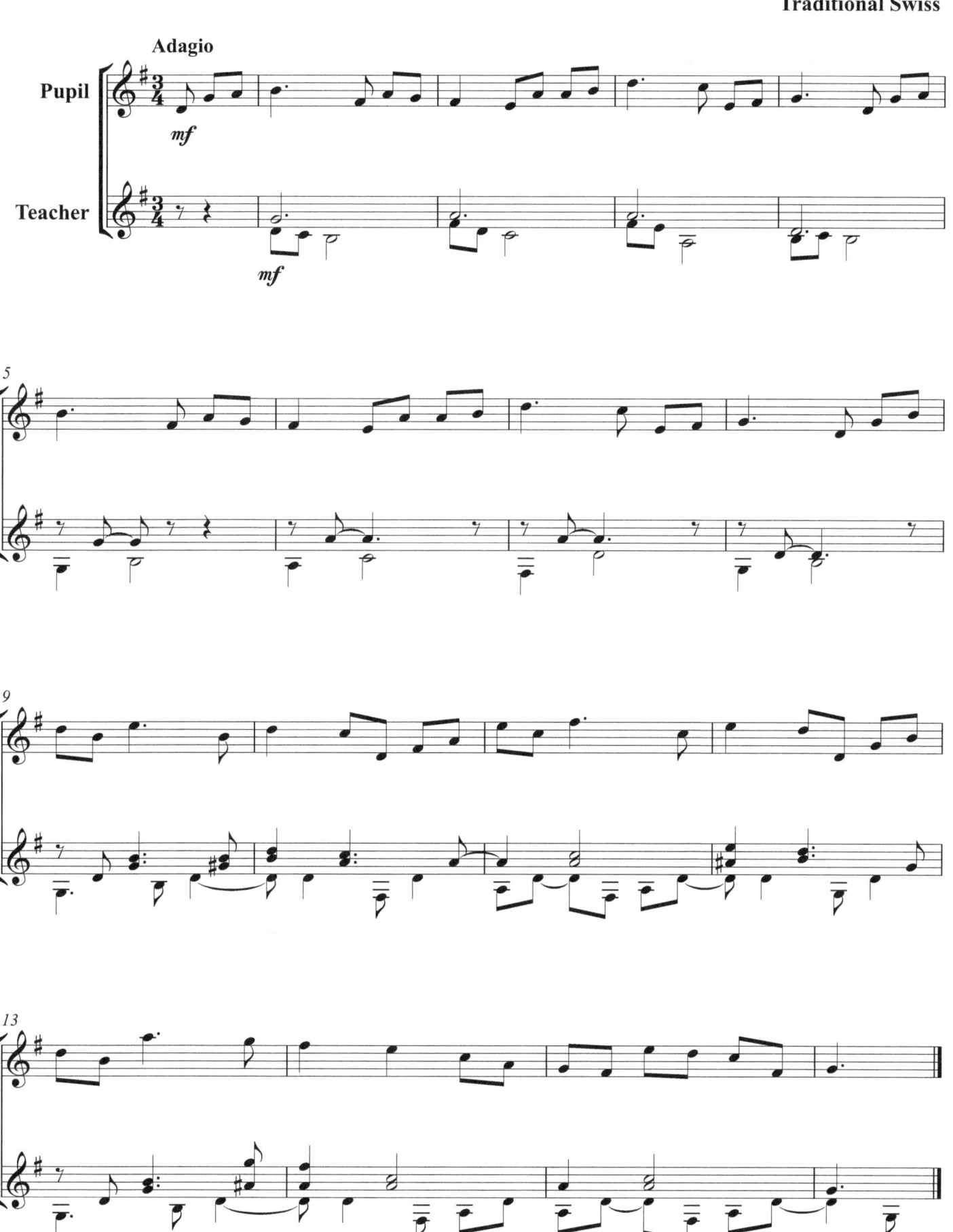

Early One Morning

Traditional English

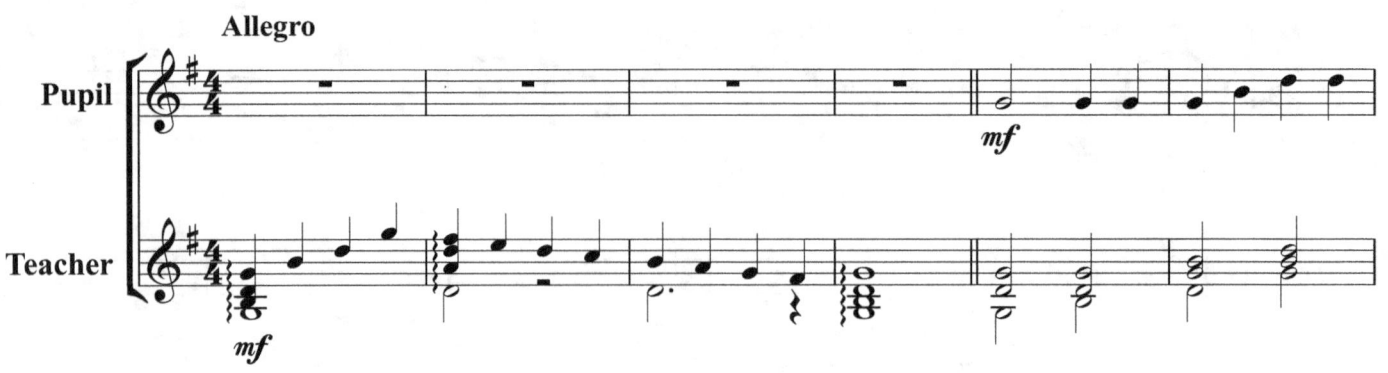

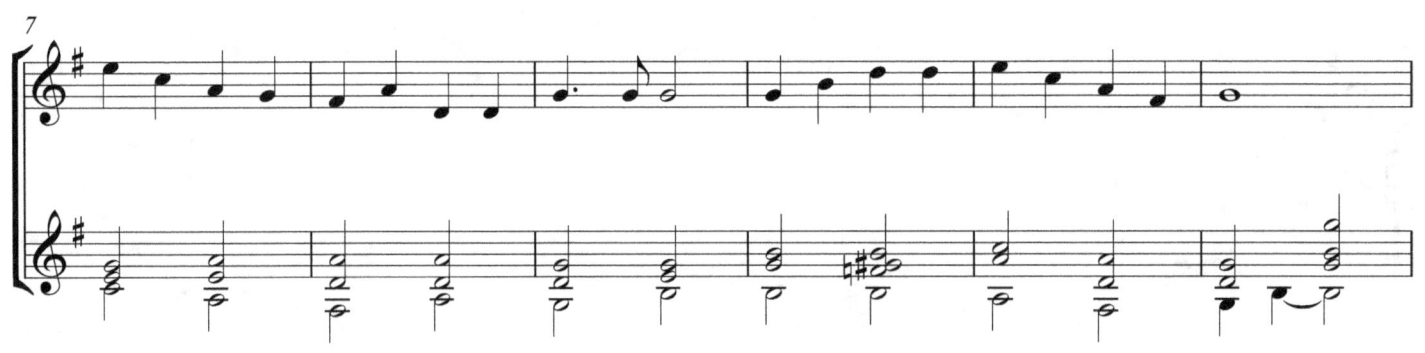

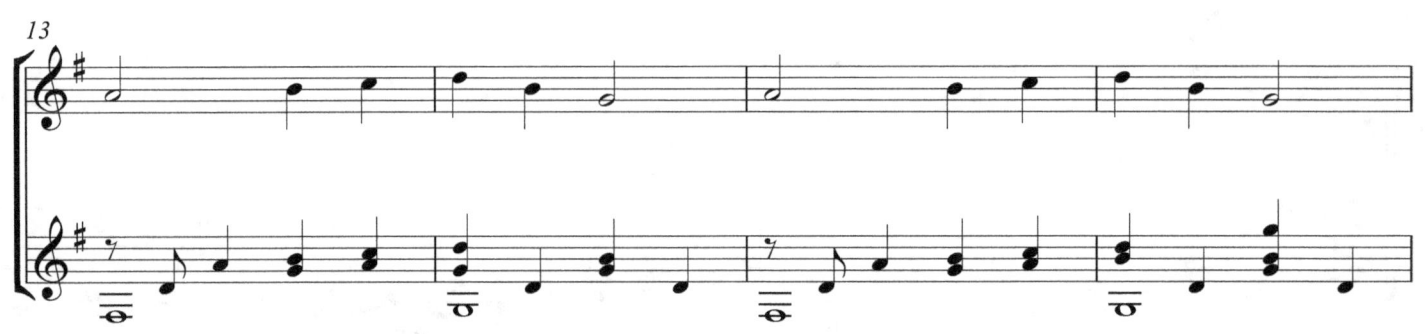

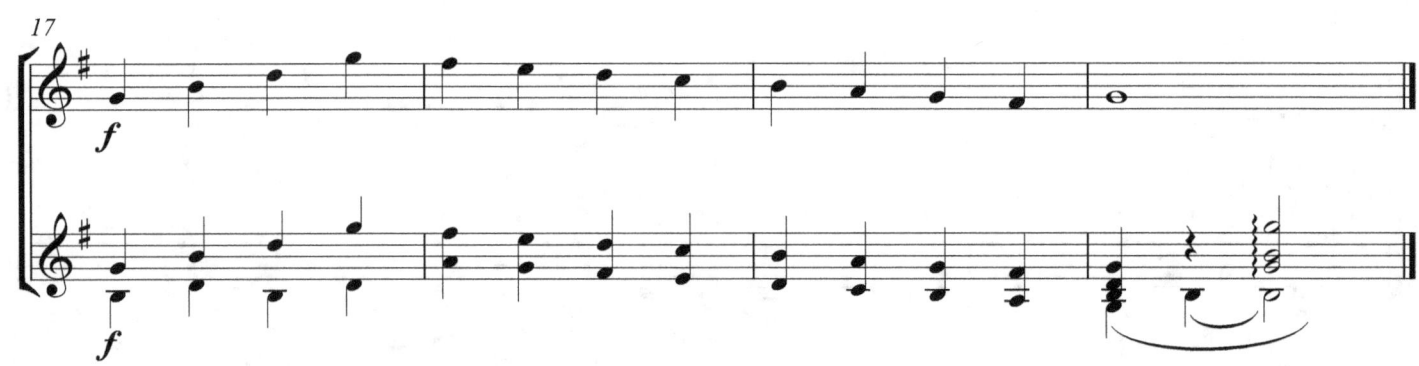

Fishermen's Evening Song

Breton Air

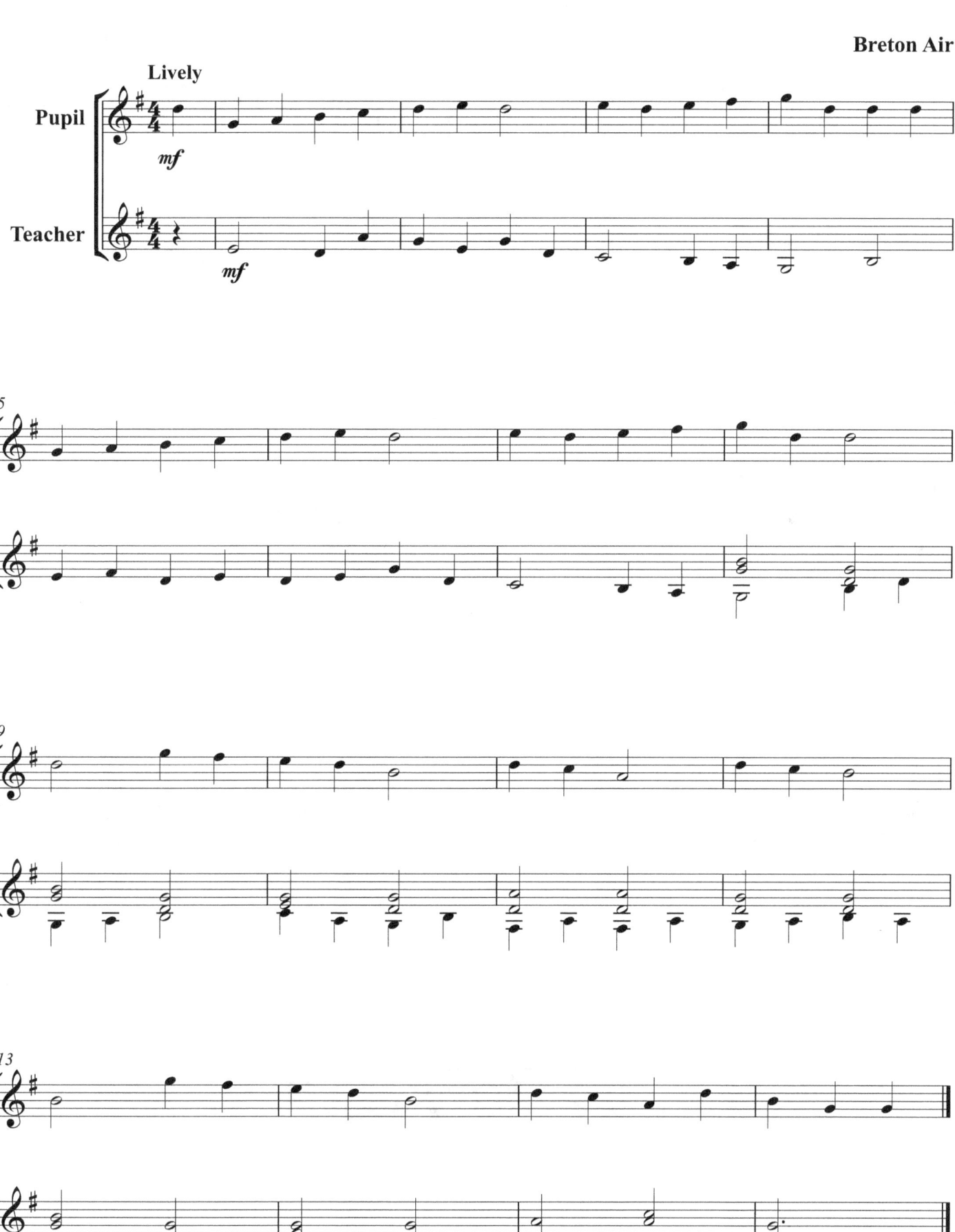

Geordie

Traditional English

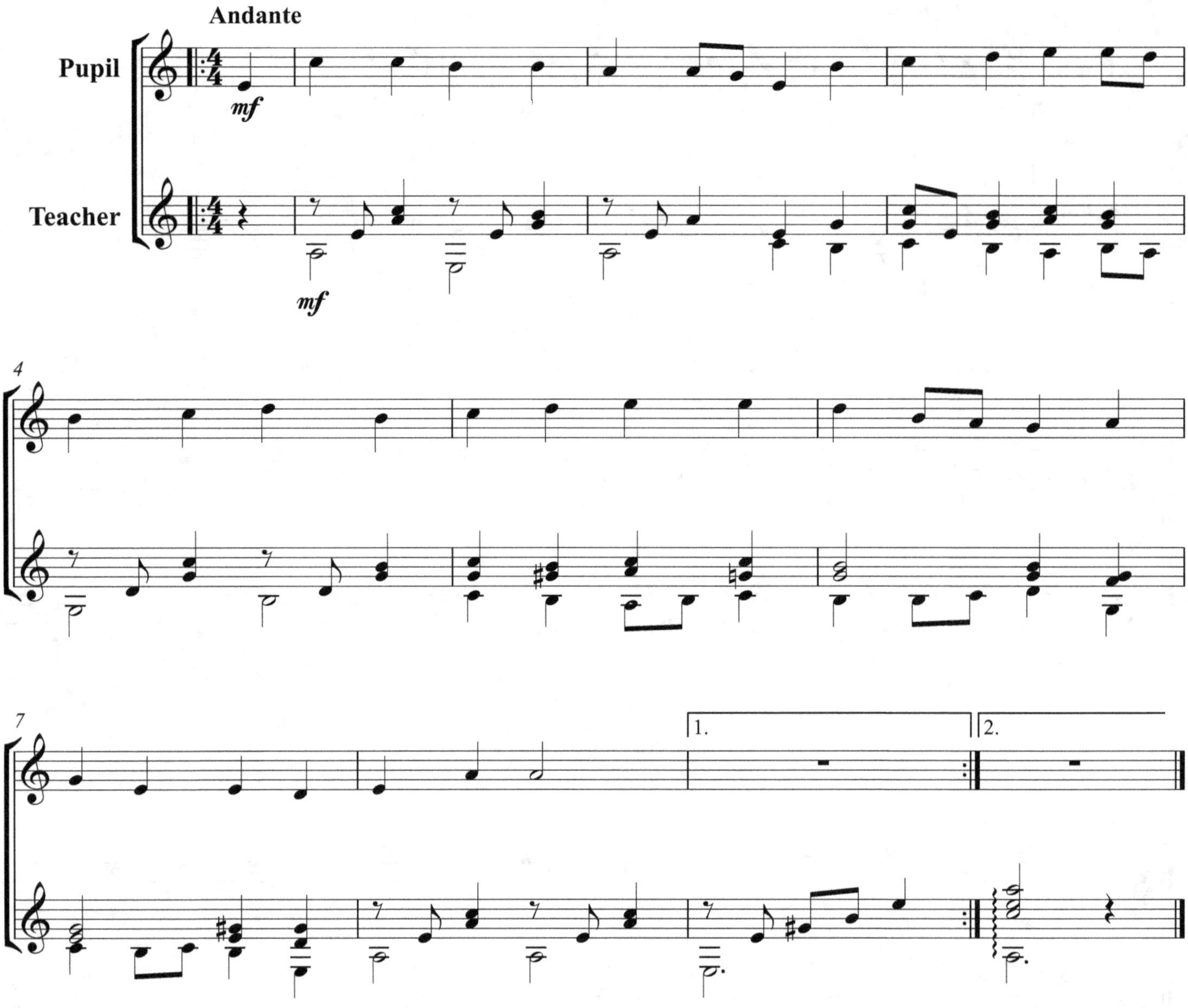

Andante

Pupil

Teacher

mf

mf

Golden Fish Swimming In The Lake

Traditional Polish

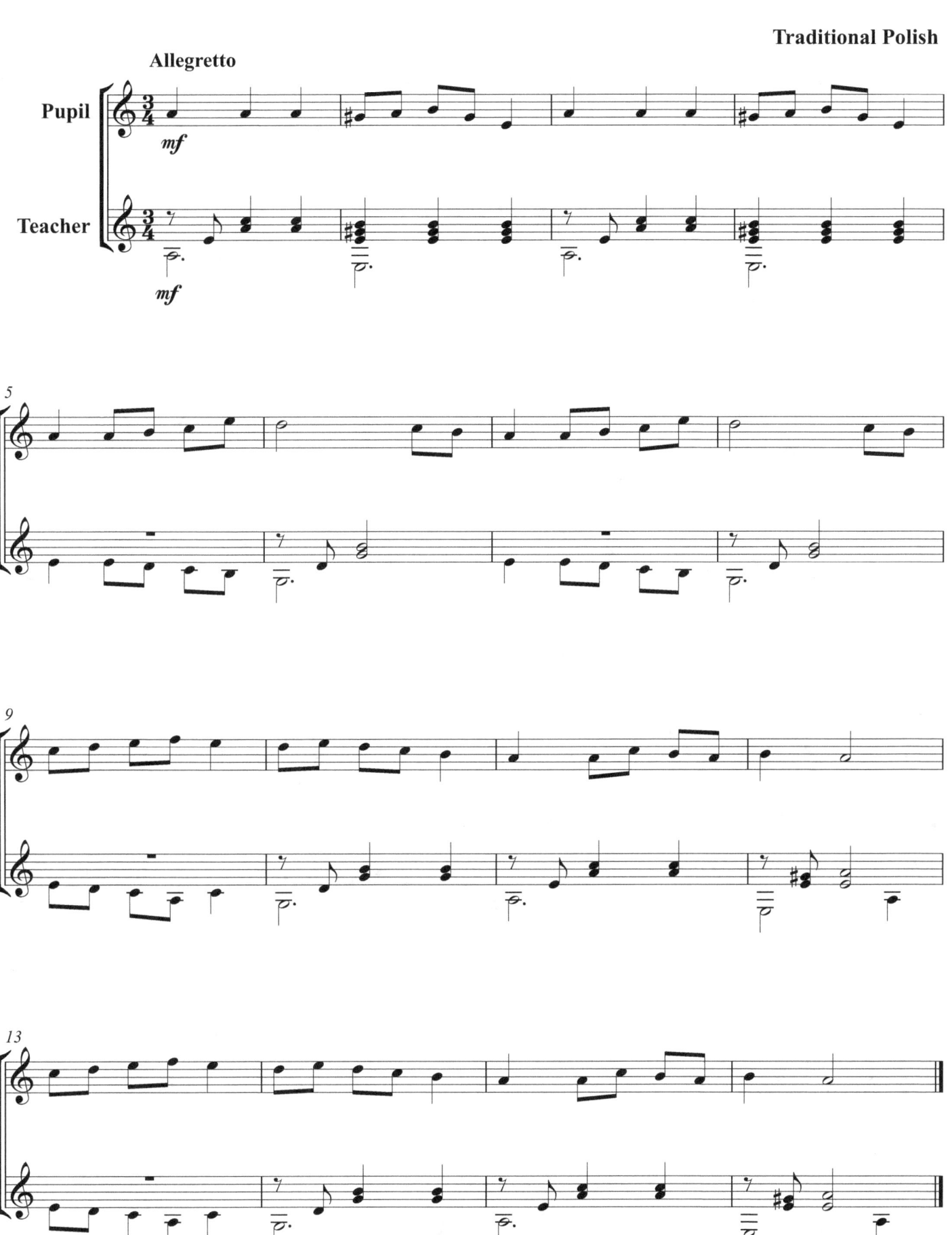

Goodnight

Traditional Czech

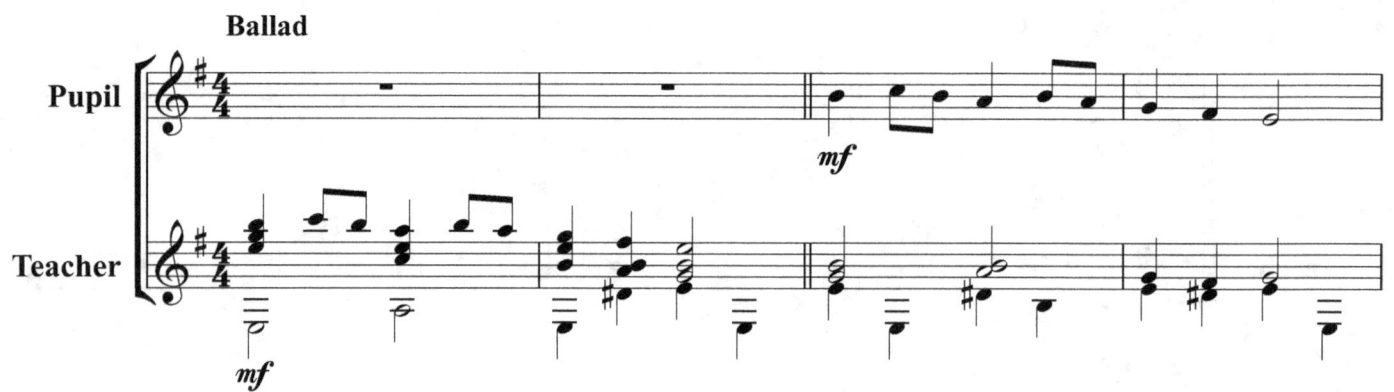

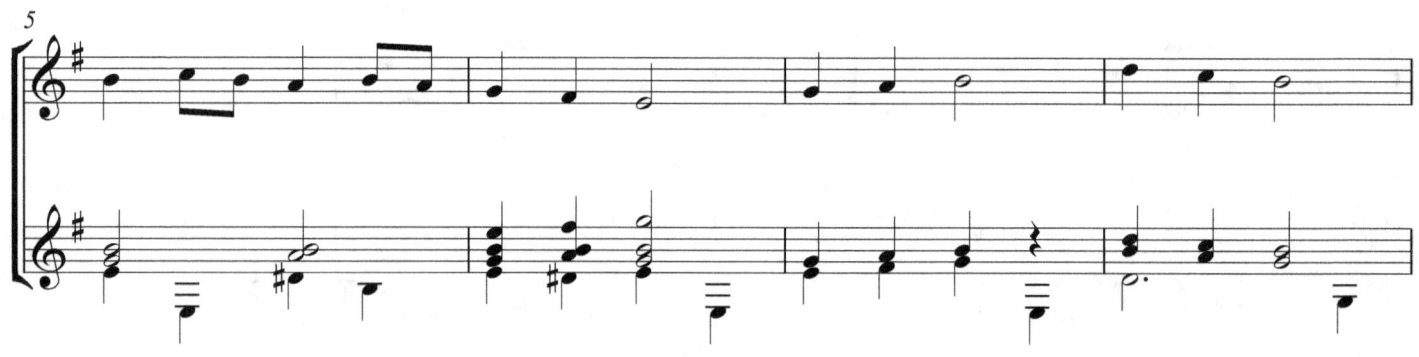

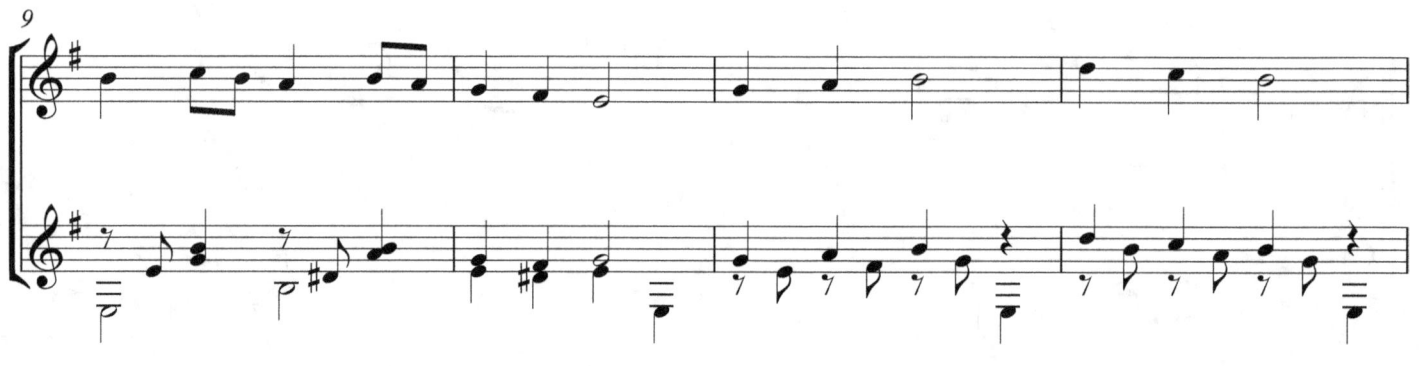

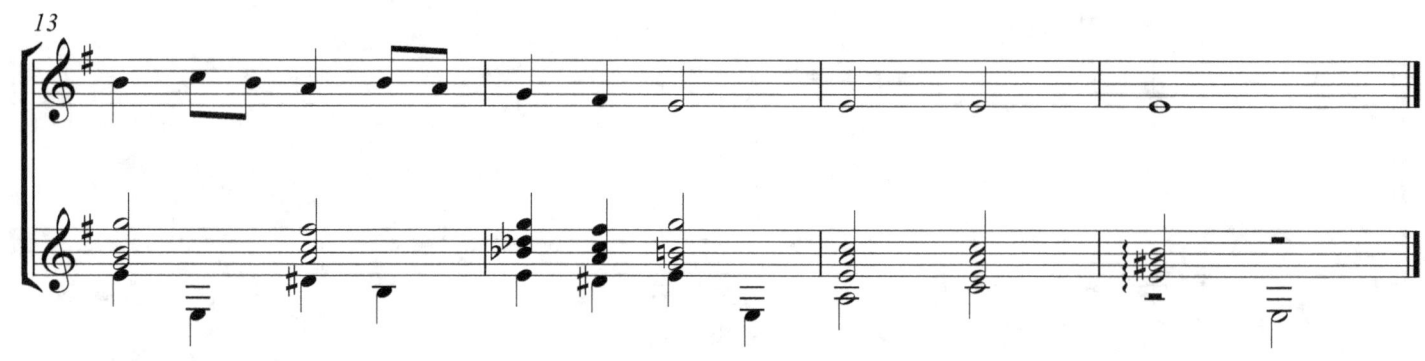

I Know Where I'm Going

Traditional Scottish

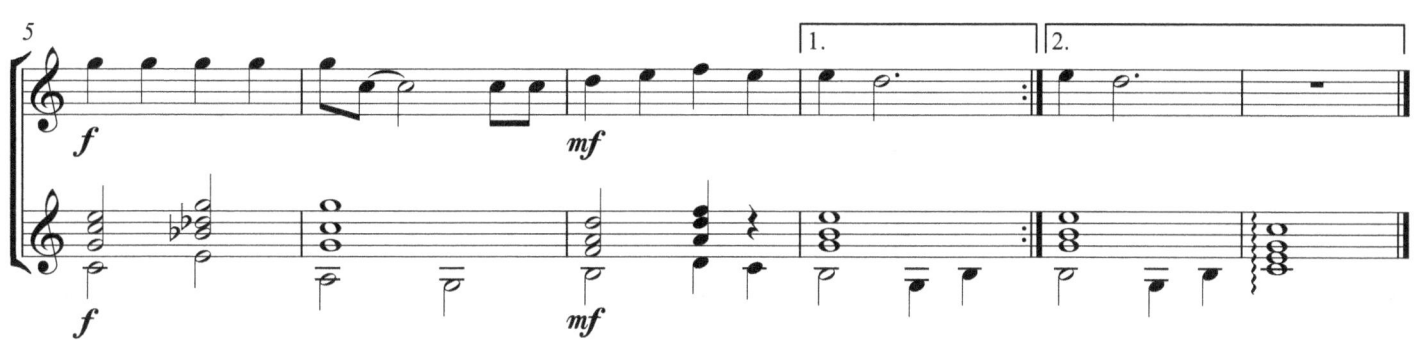

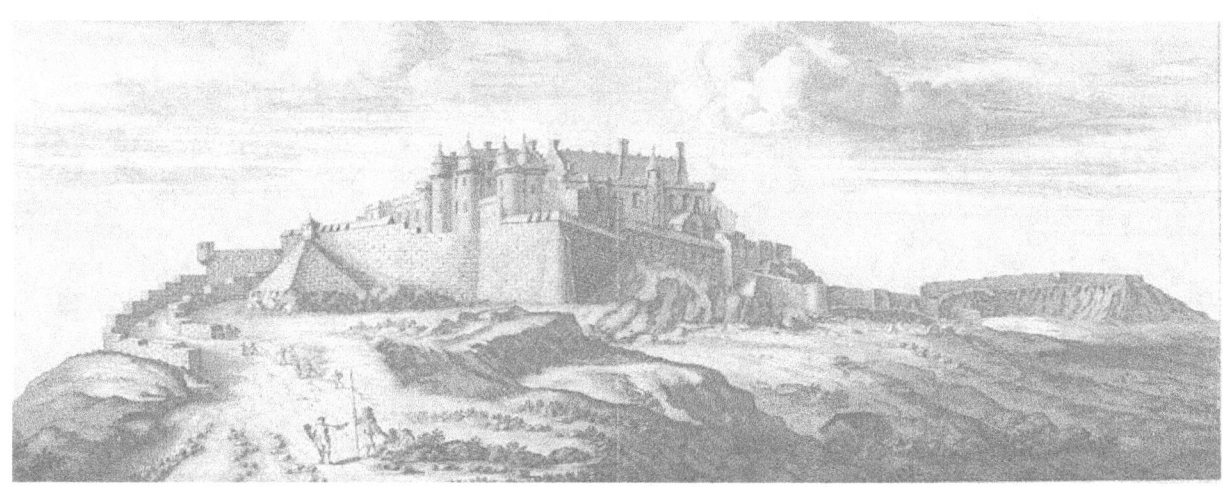

Stirling Castle, Scotland, 1693

I'm Seventeen Come Sunday

Traditional English

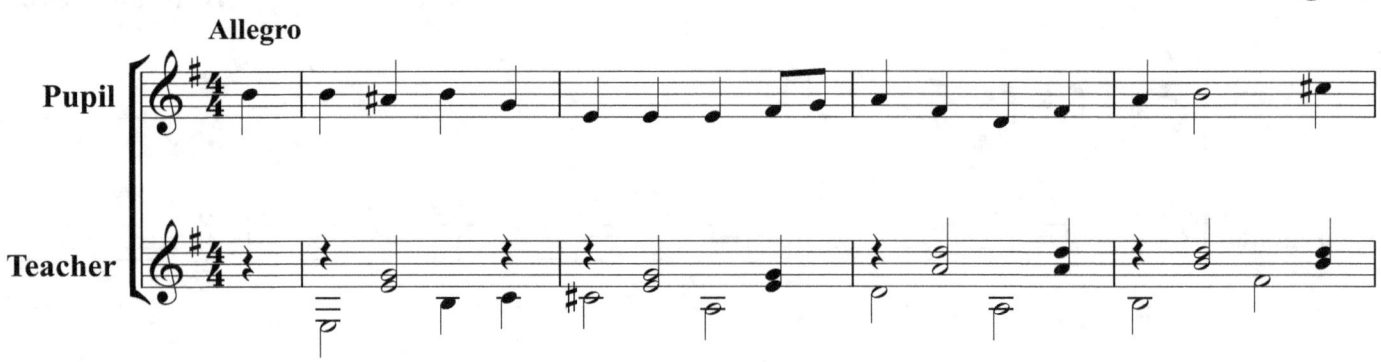

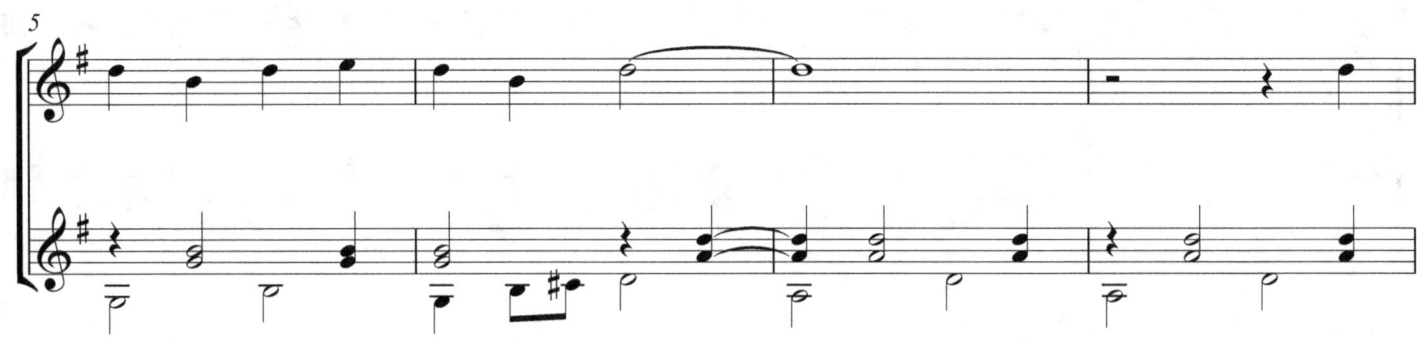

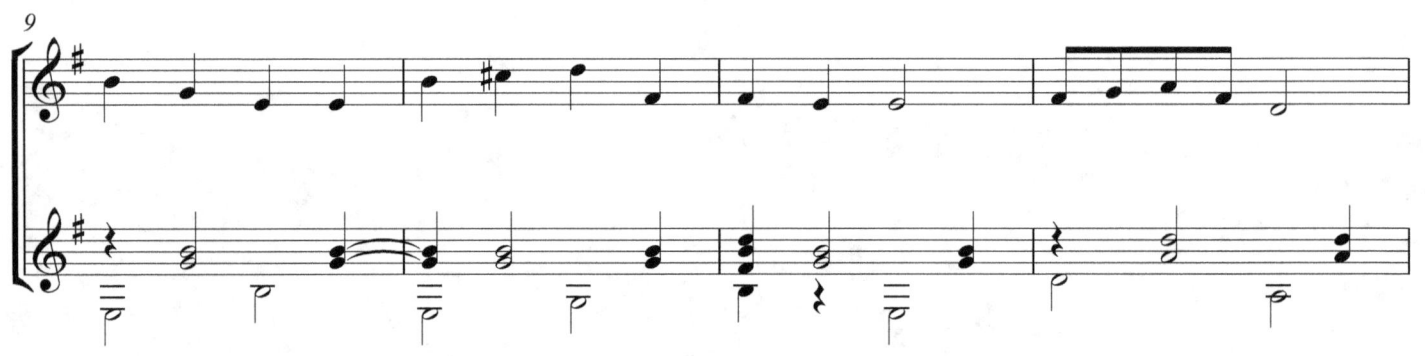

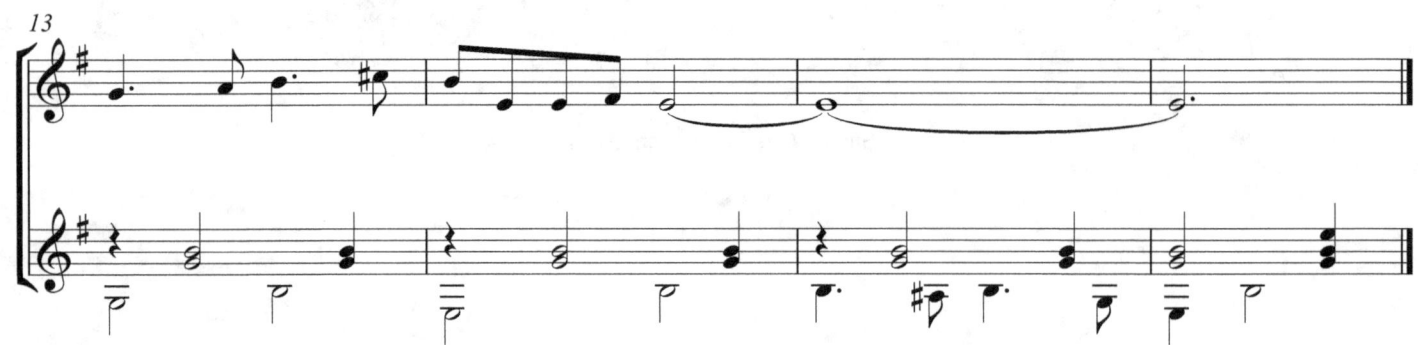

I Would Soothe You

Traditional Uist

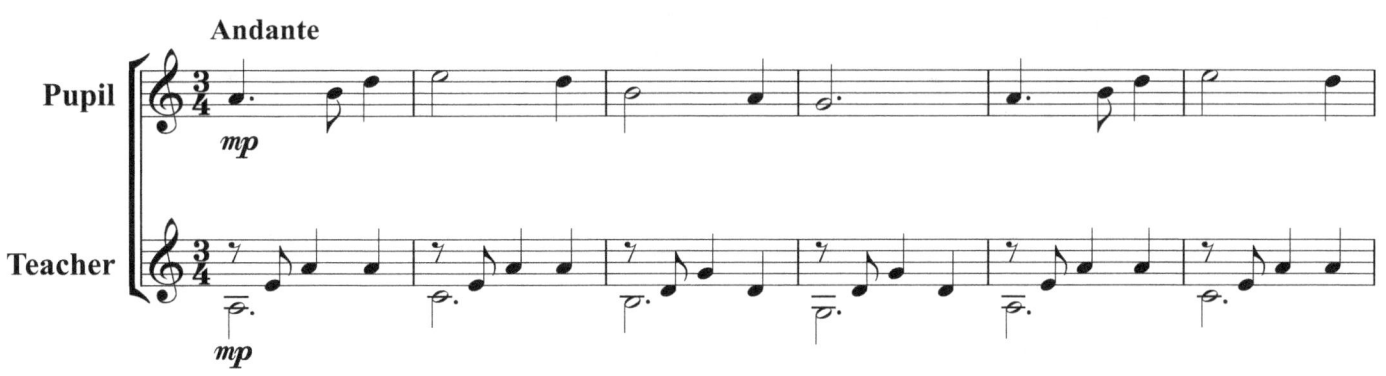

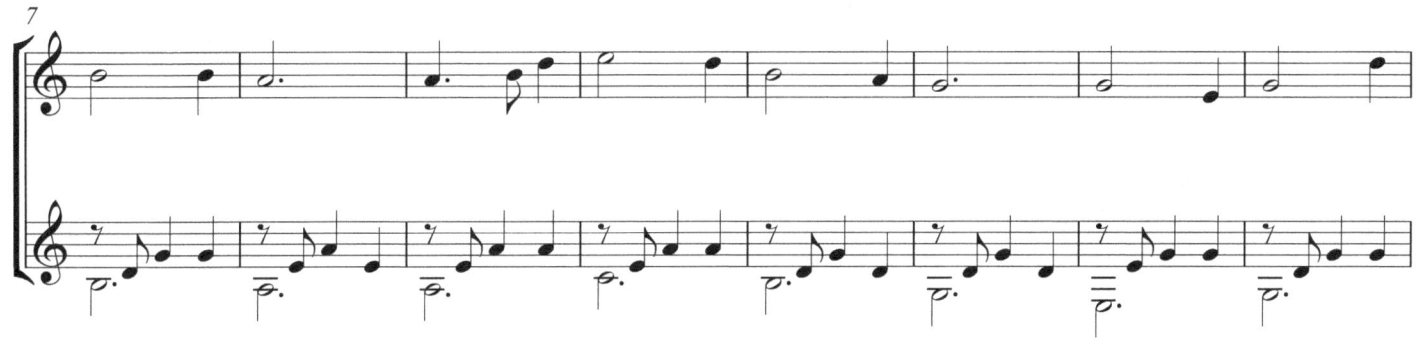

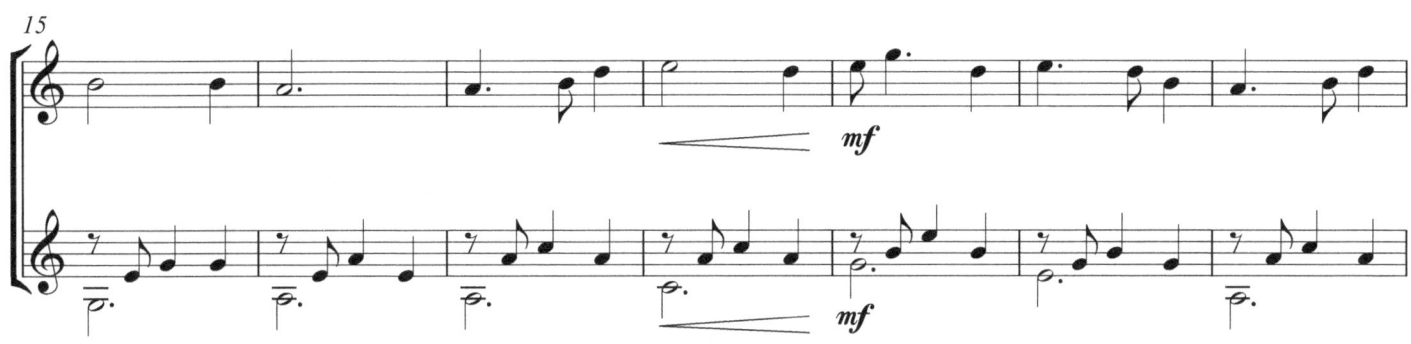

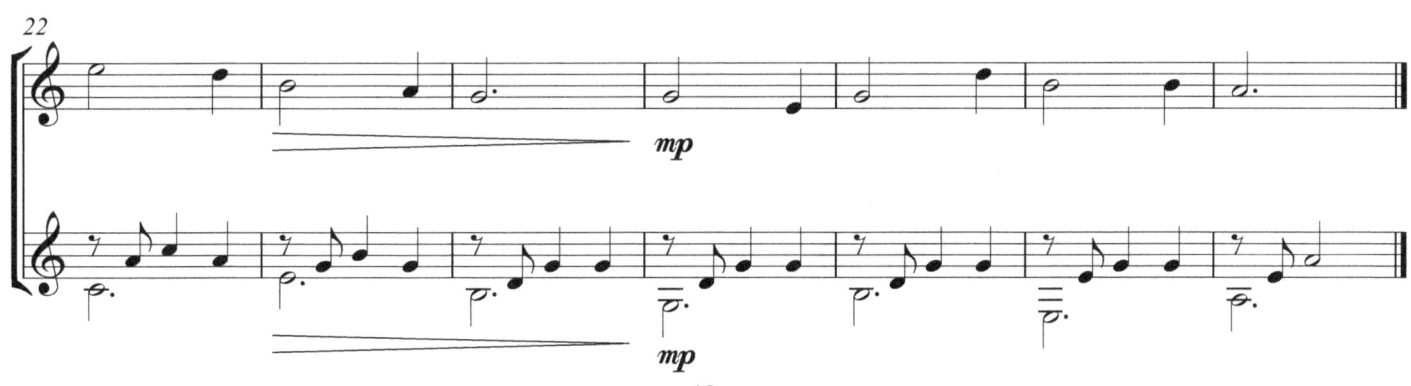

Poor Old Horse

Traditional English

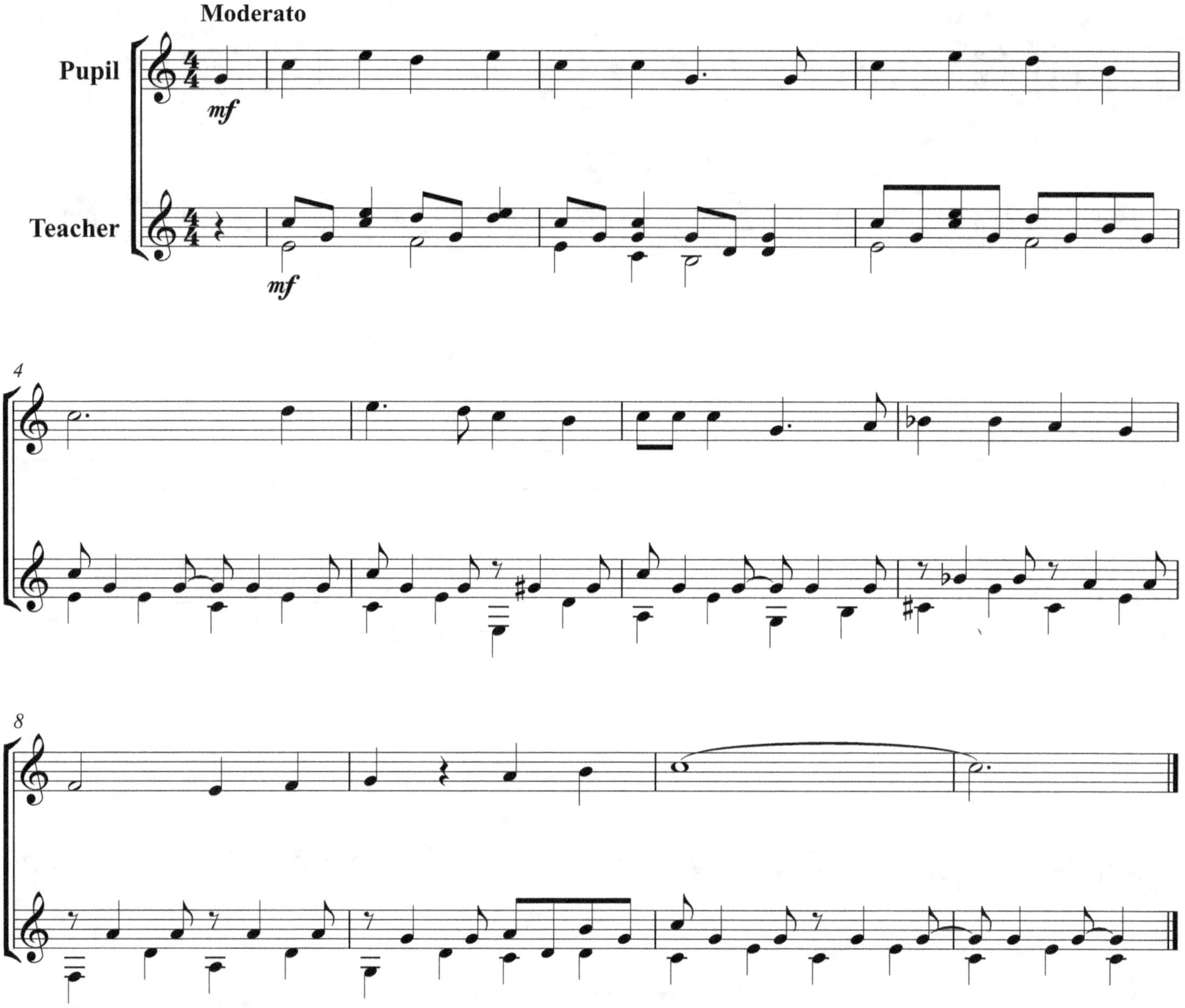

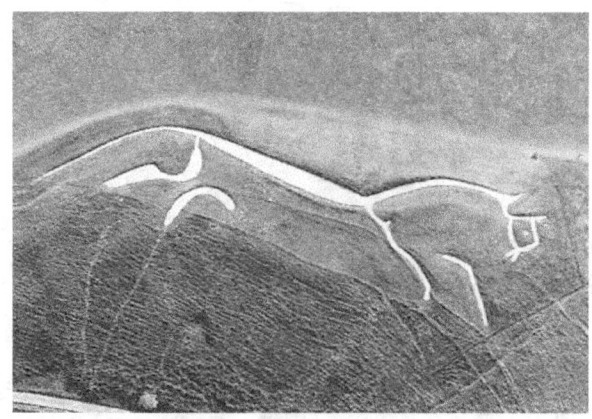

Uffington White Horse. Bronze Age Hill Figure, Uffington, Oxfordshire

Robin Redbreast

Traditional Welsh

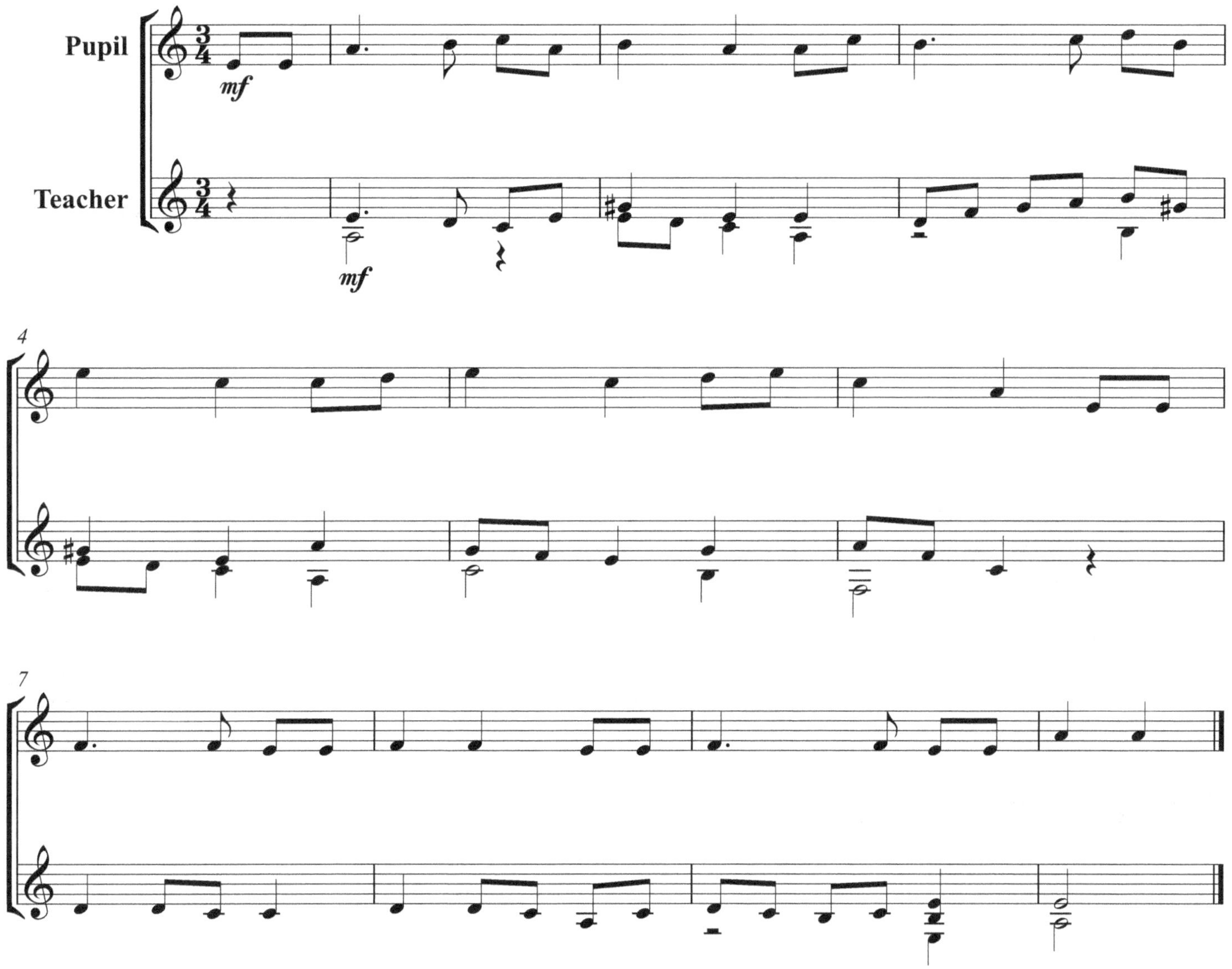

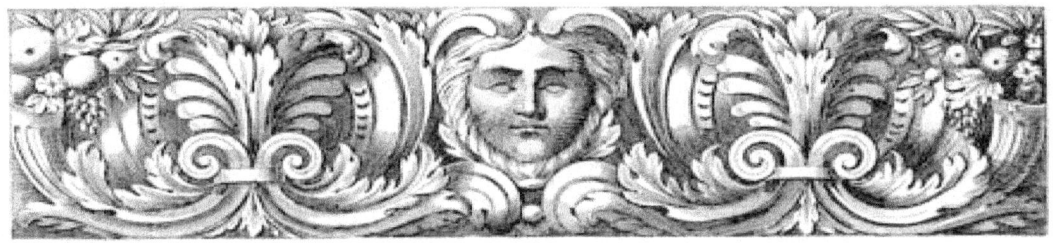

Megan's Fair Daughter

Traditional Welsh

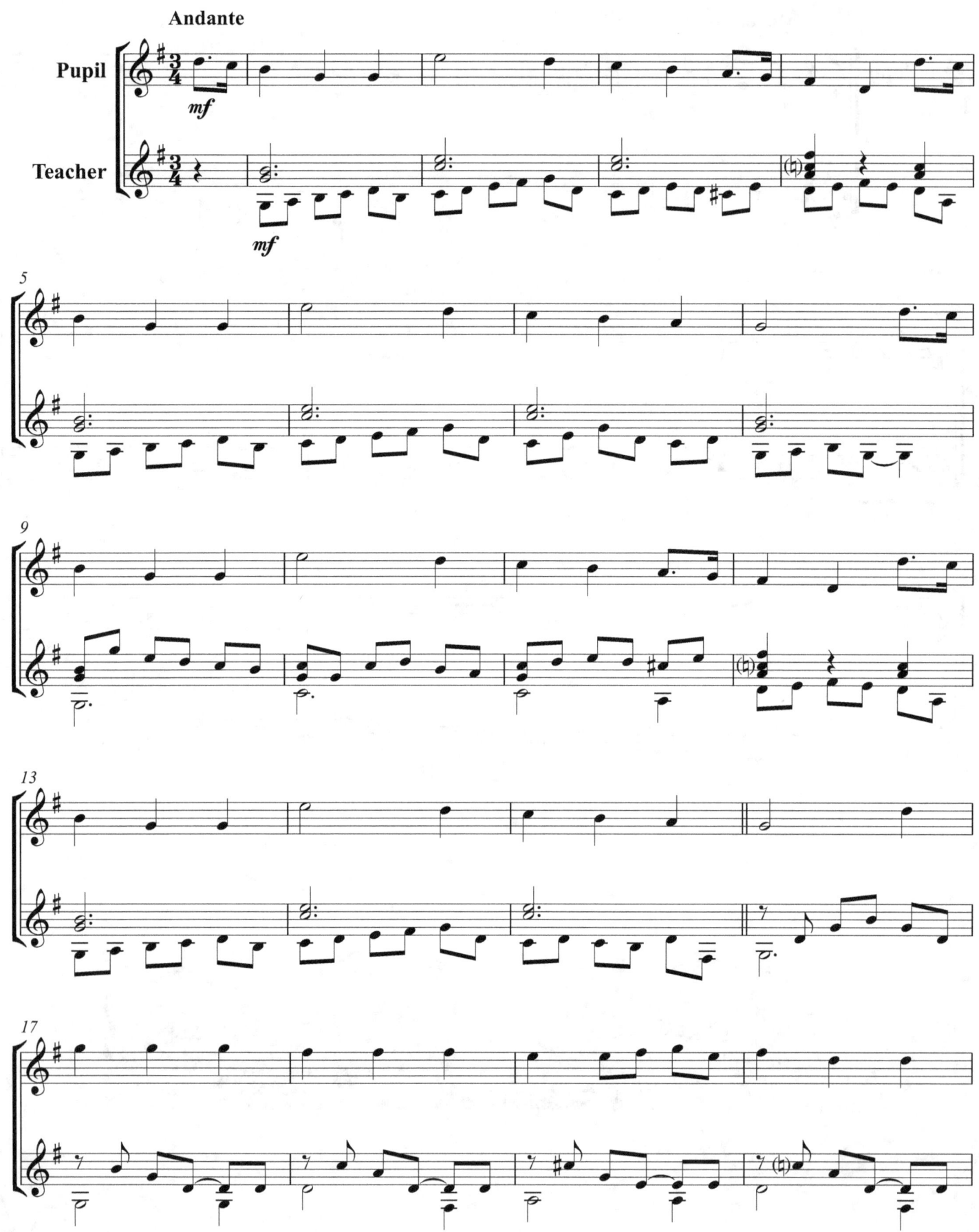

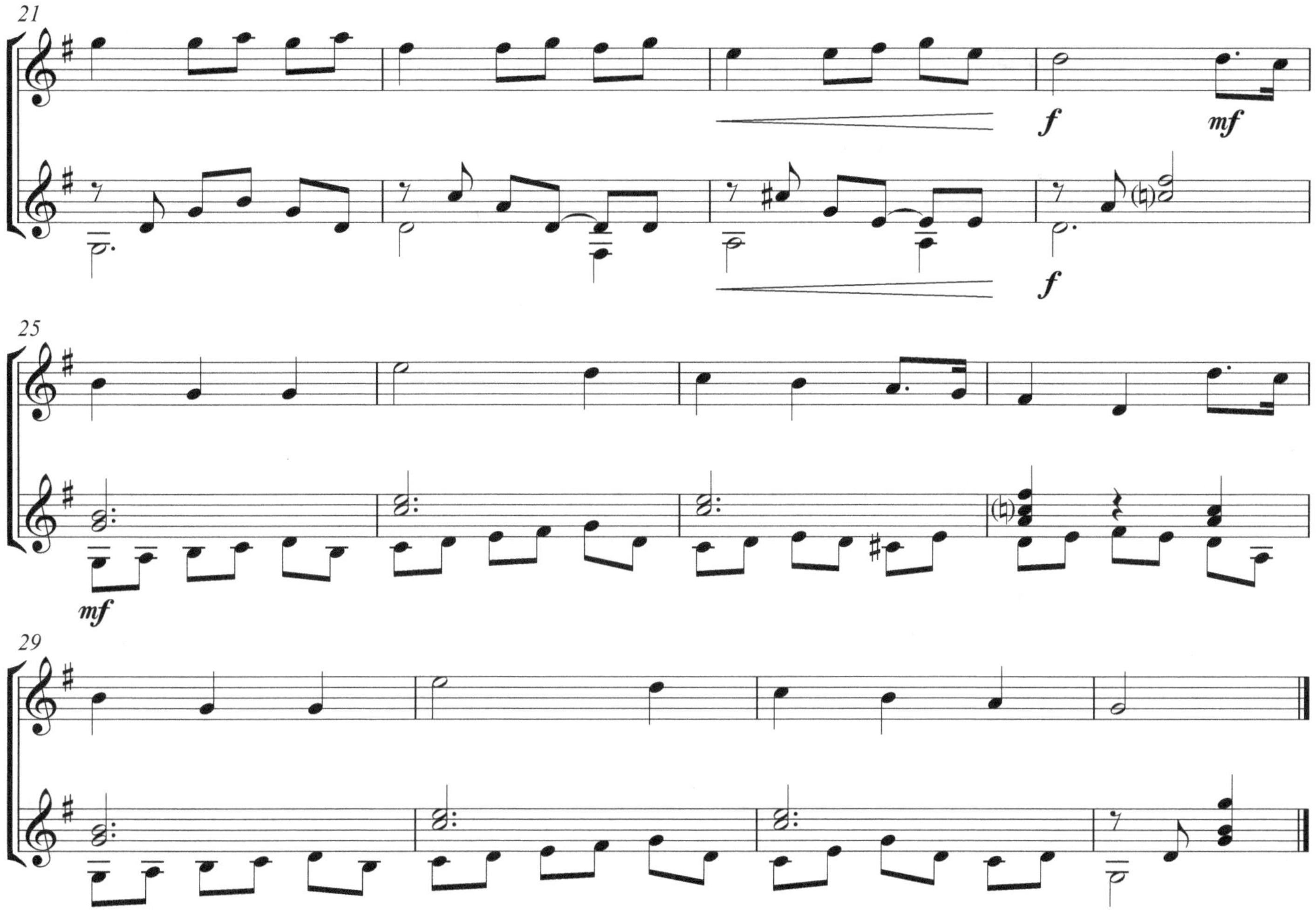

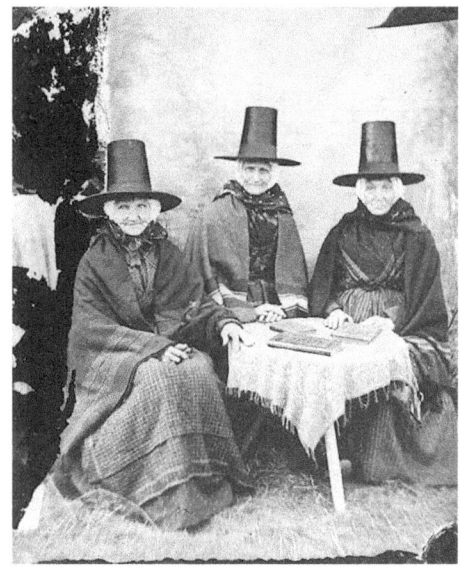

Traditional Welsh Costume

O Vermeland

A.Fryxell

Traditional Swedish

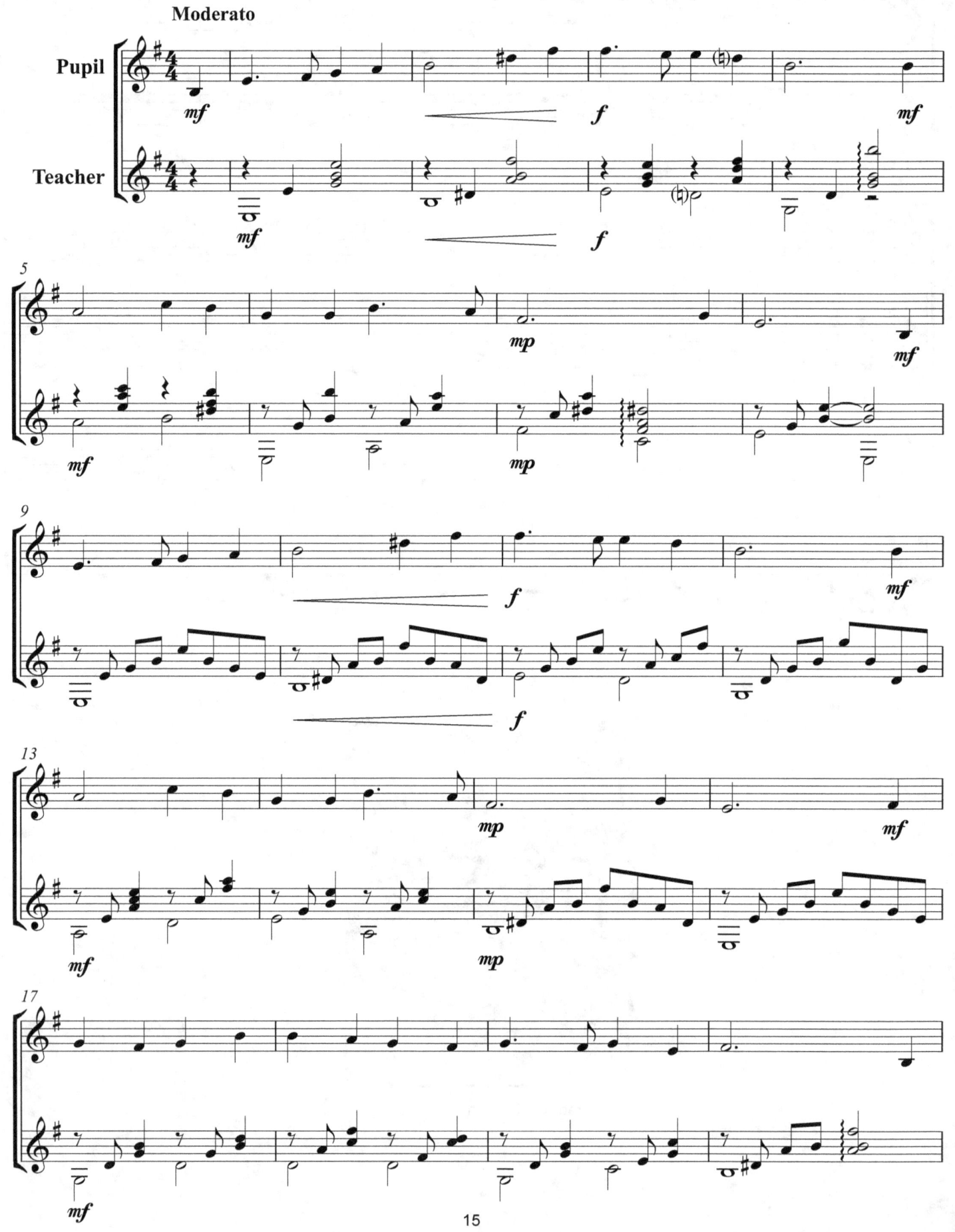

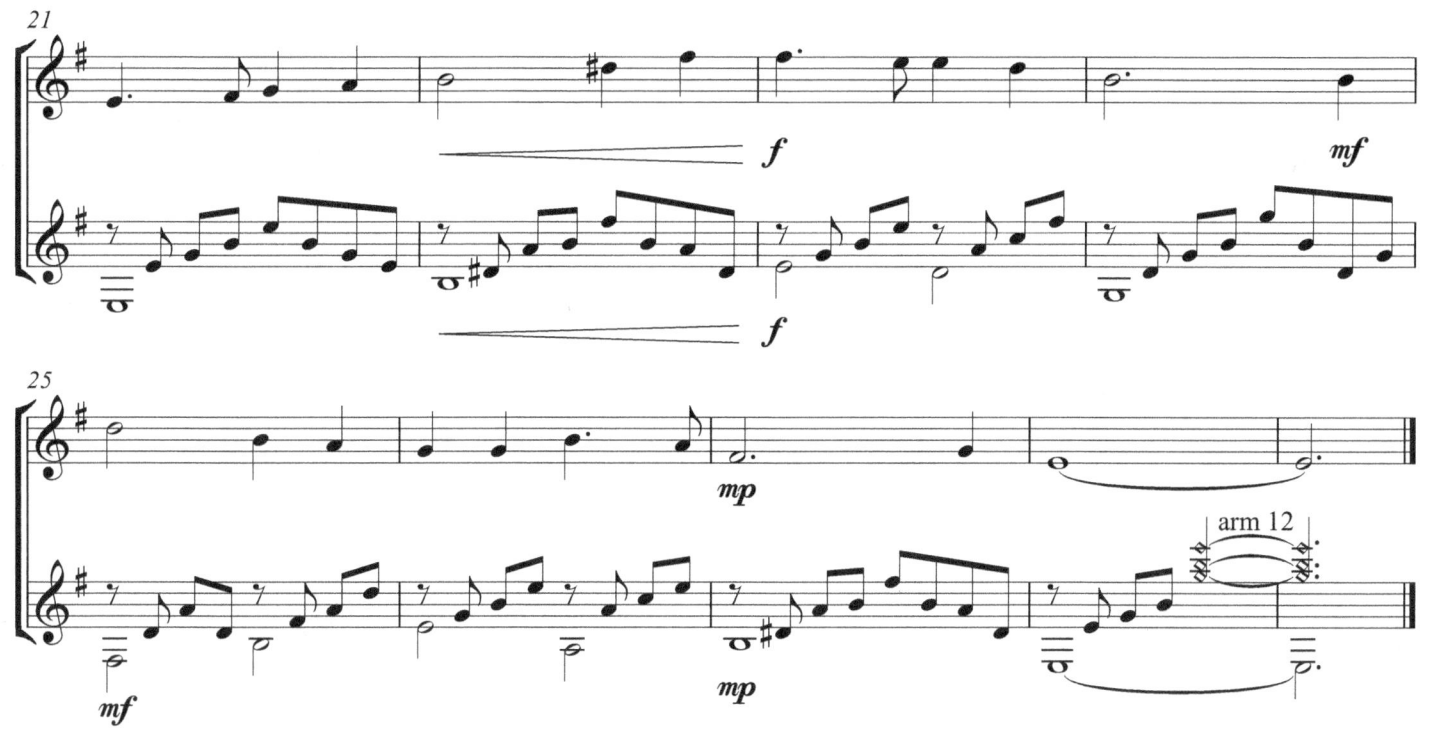

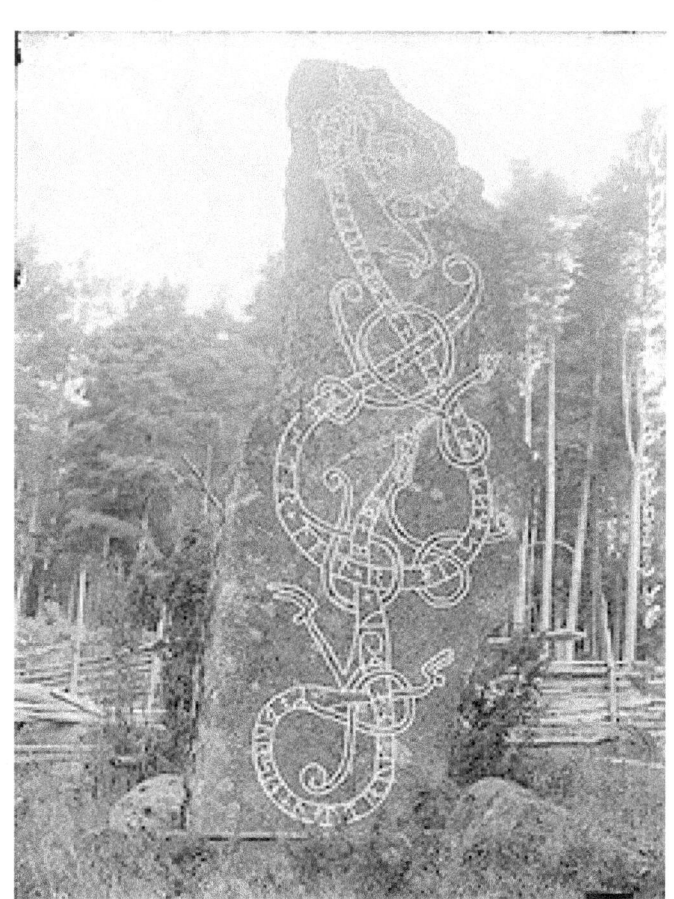

Nasby Runestone, Uppland, Sweden

Santa Lucia

Folk Song of Naples

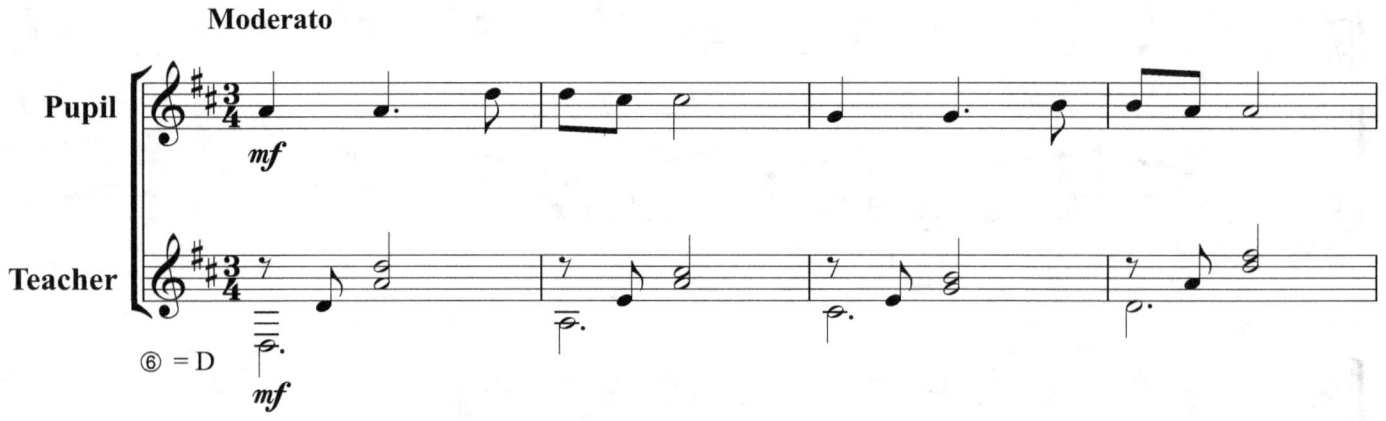

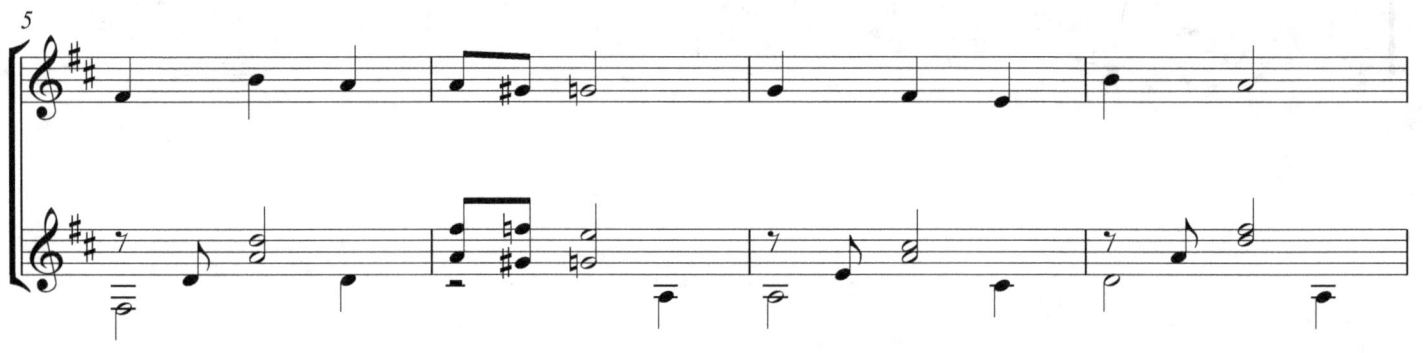

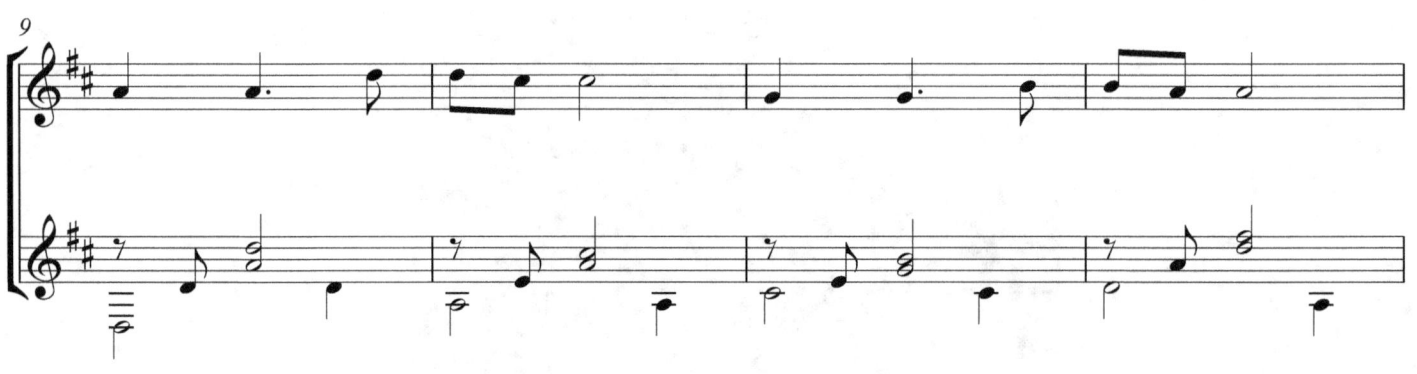

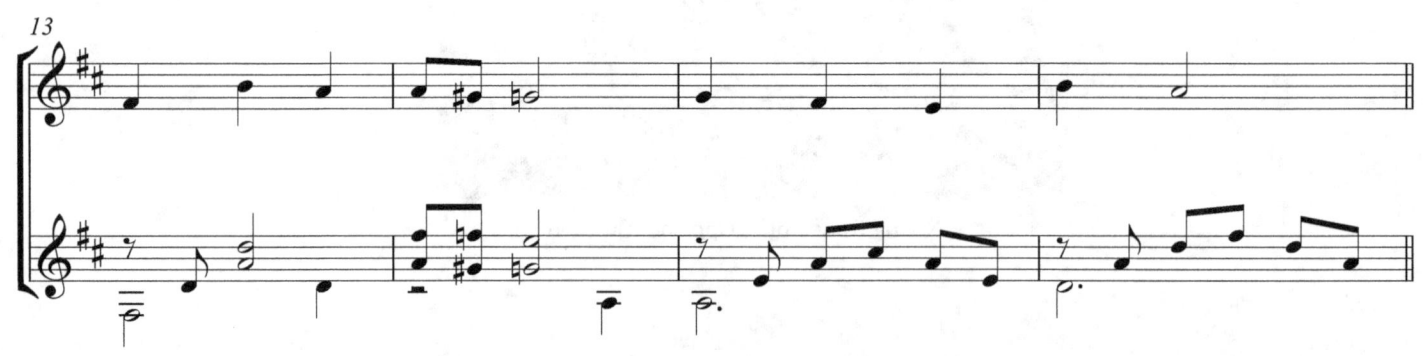

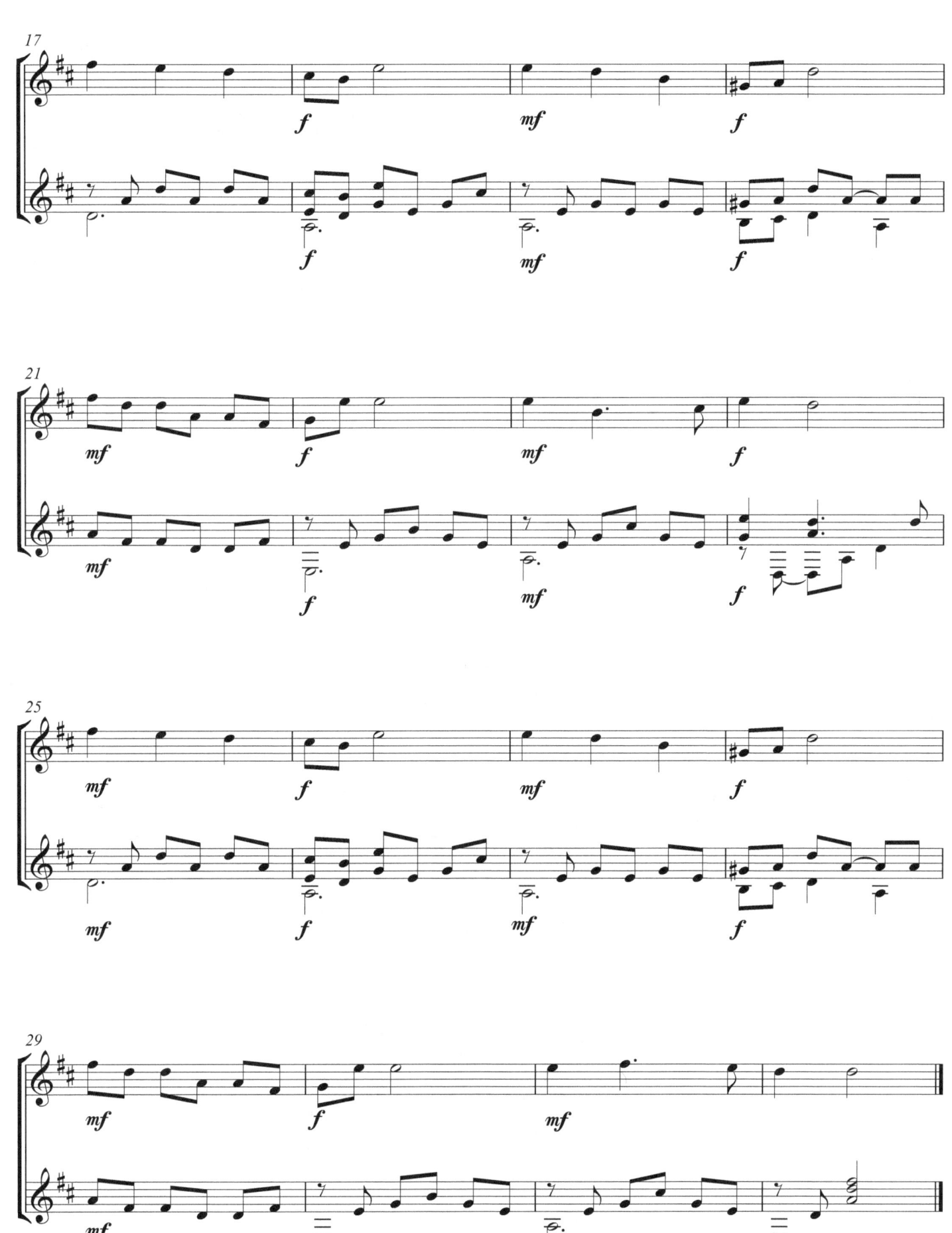

Shoes Of Shining Leather

Traditional Hungarian

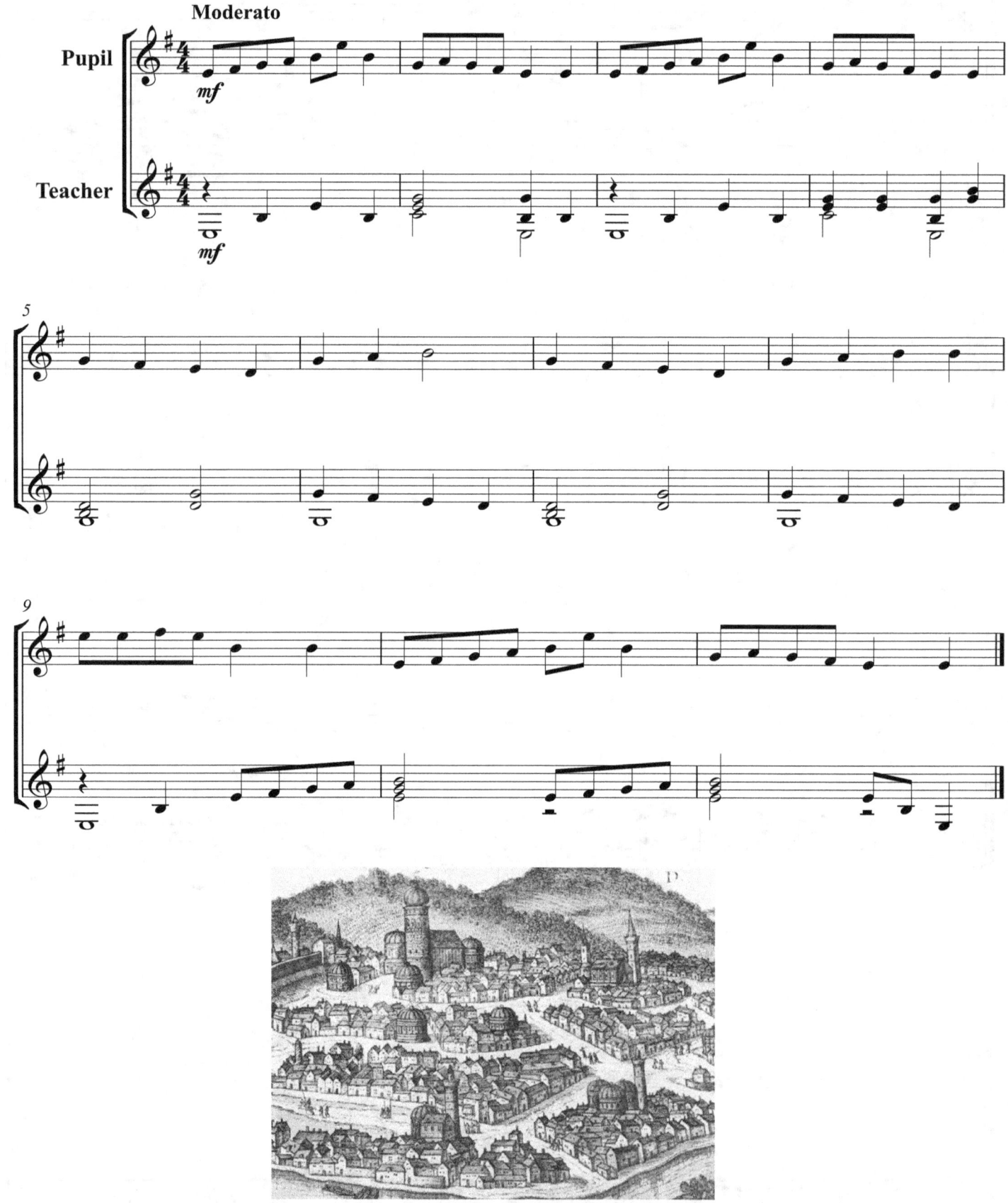

Budapest, Hungary, 1617

19

Shule Aroon

Traditional Irish

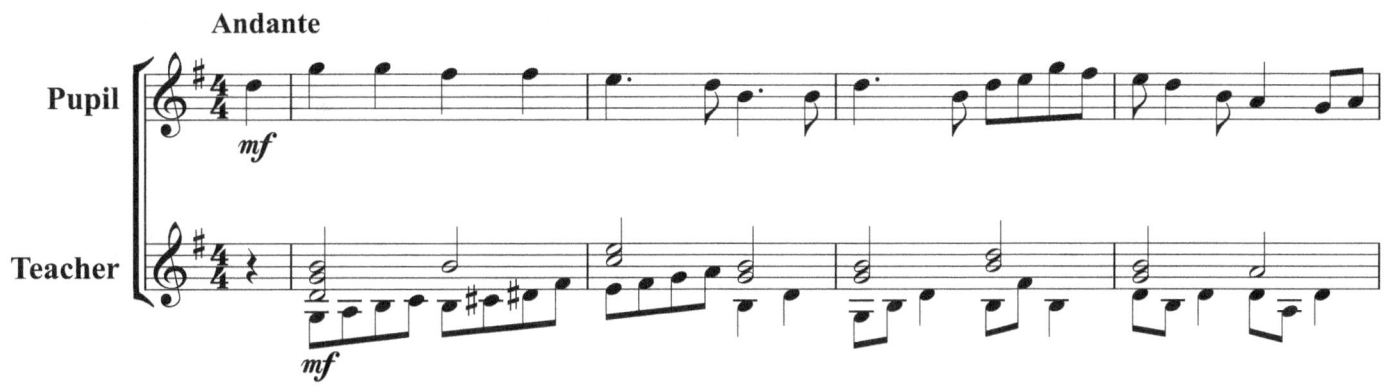

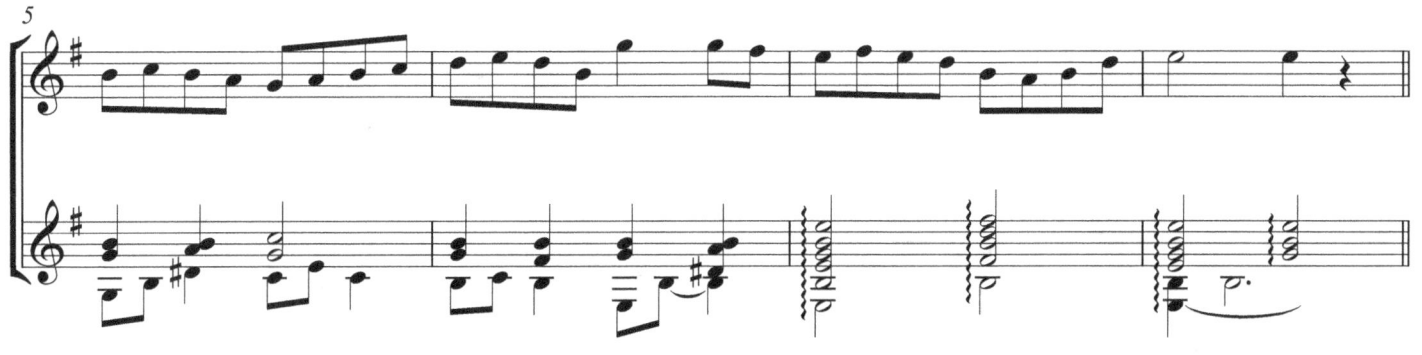

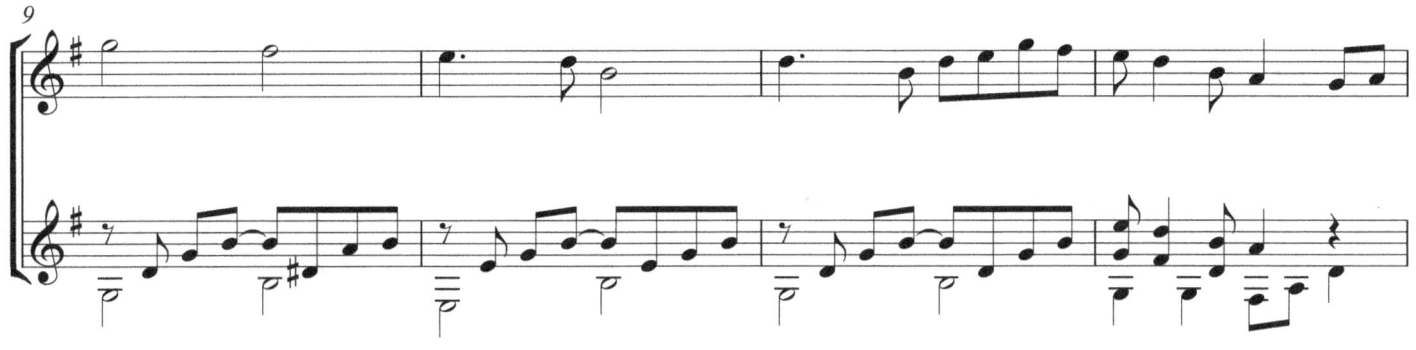

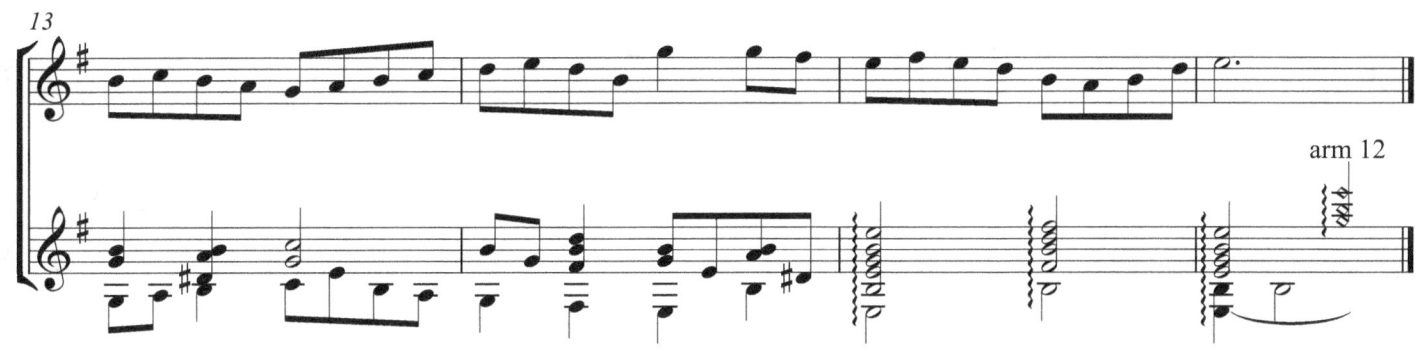

The Old Home

Folk Song of the Low Countries

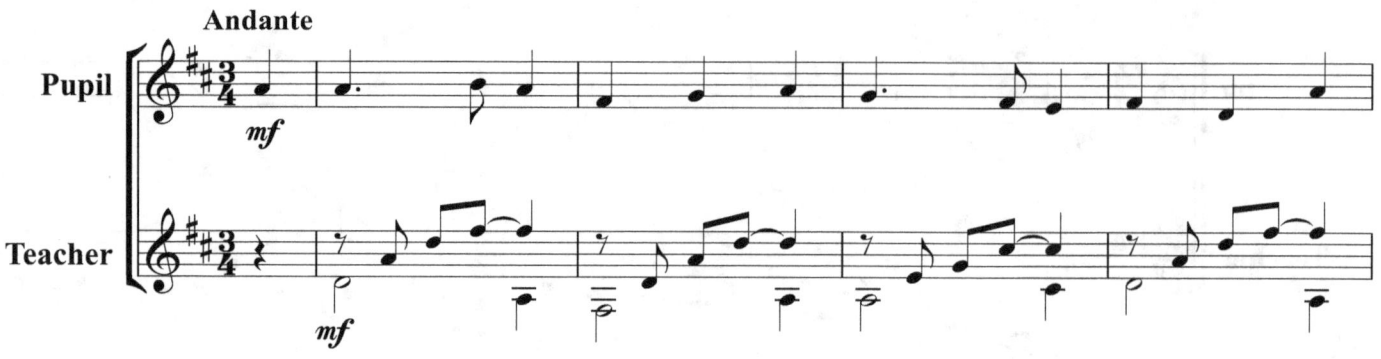

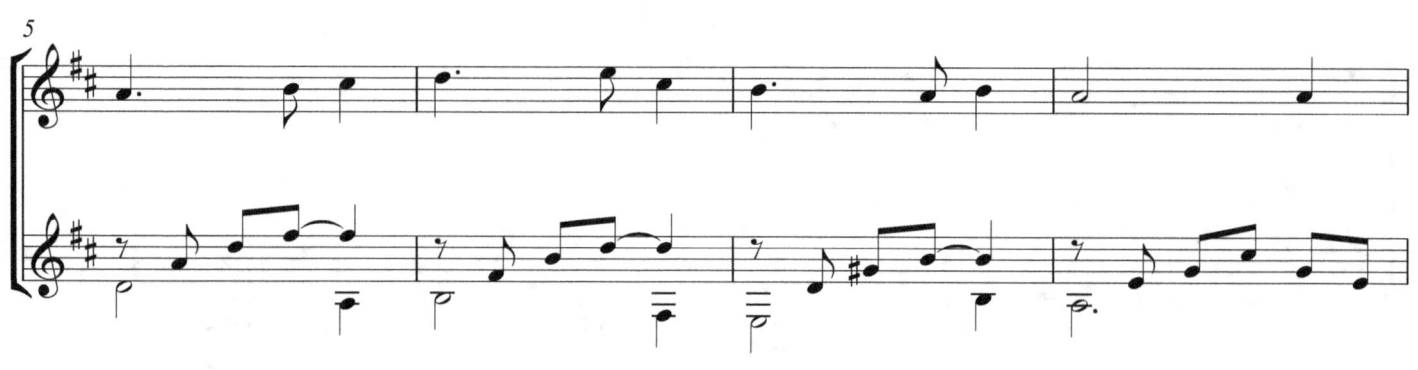

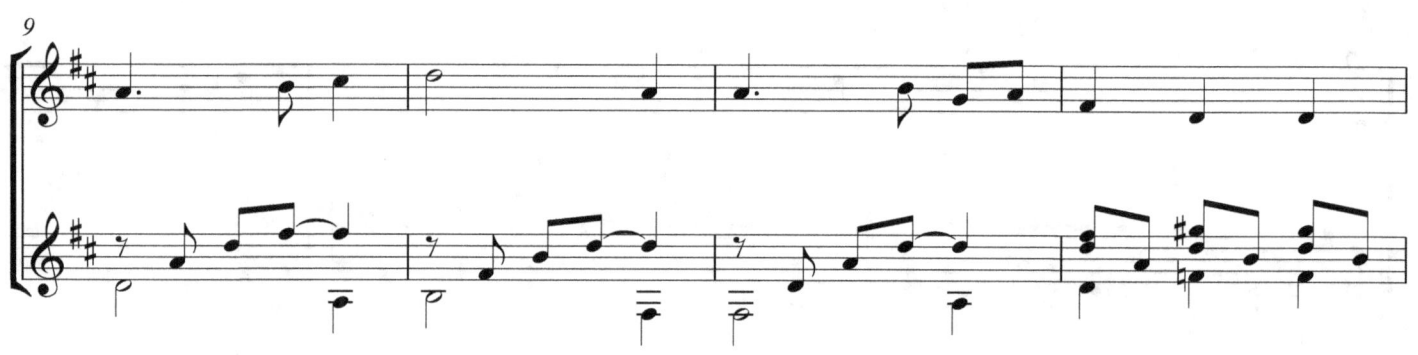

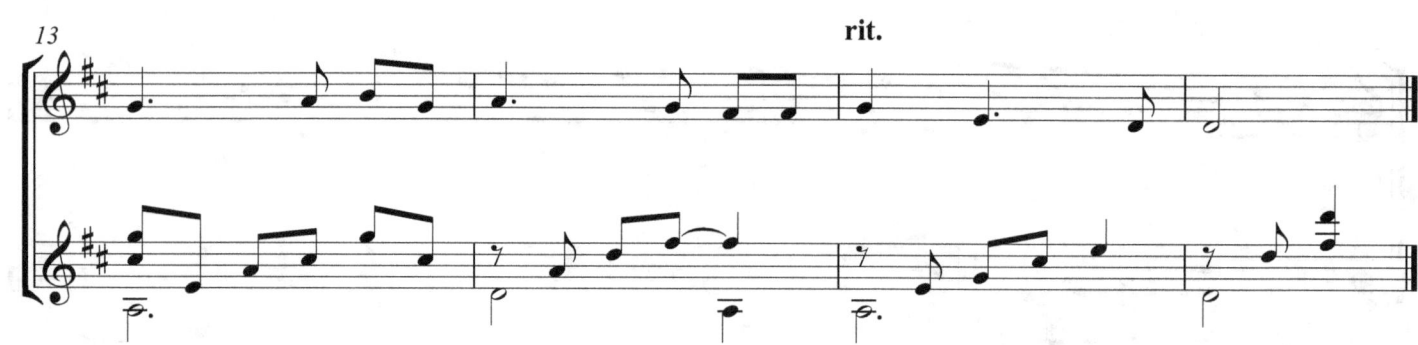

There Came a Little Stranger

Old French Carol

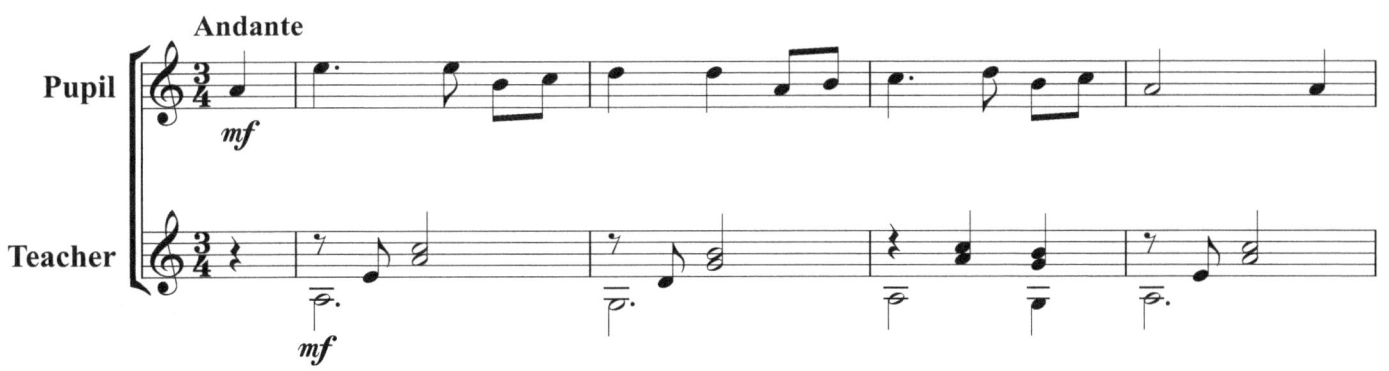

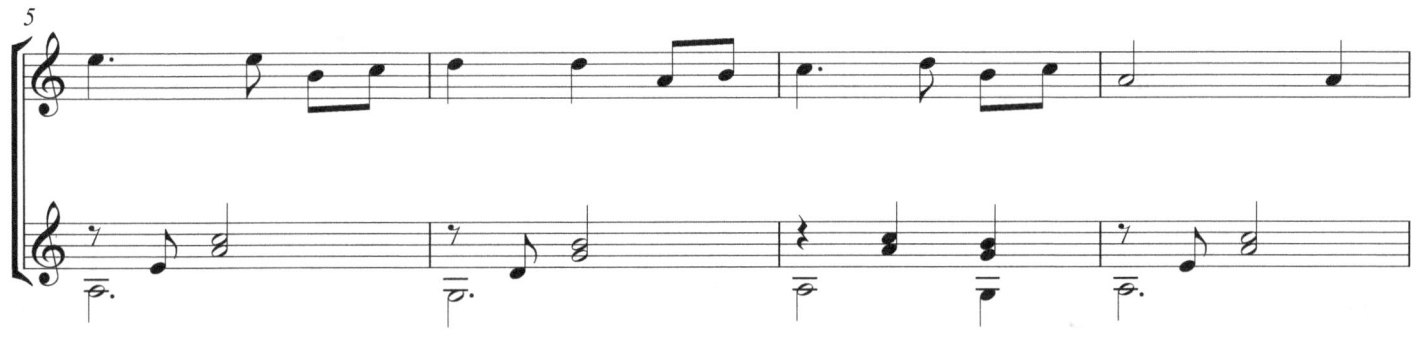

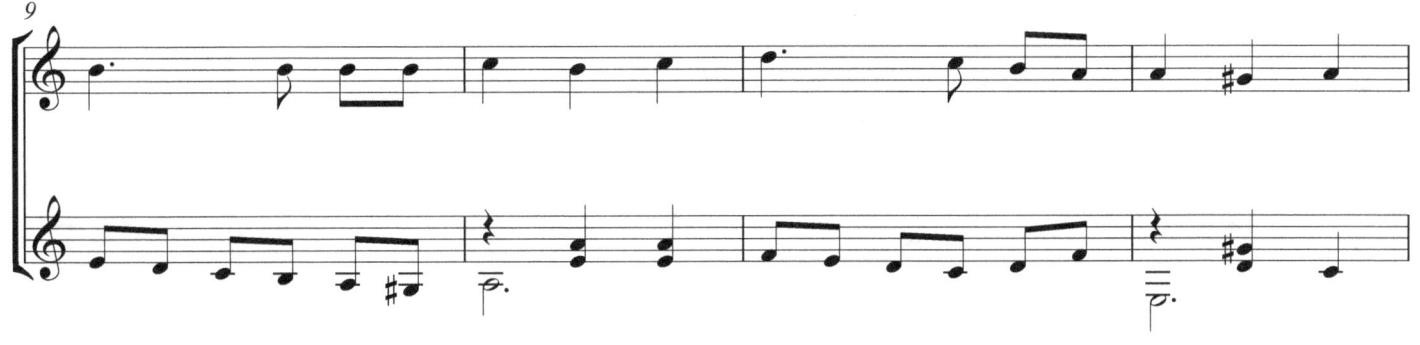

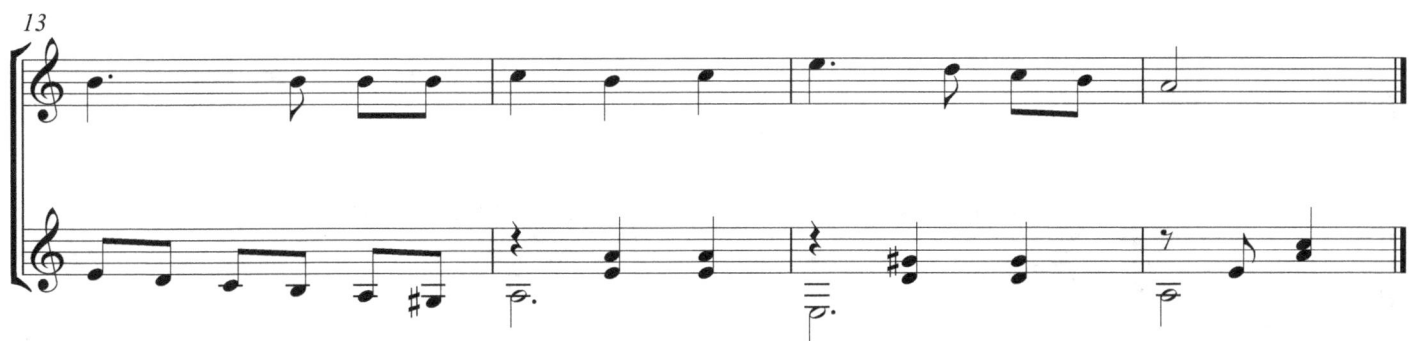

The Lorelei

Traditional German

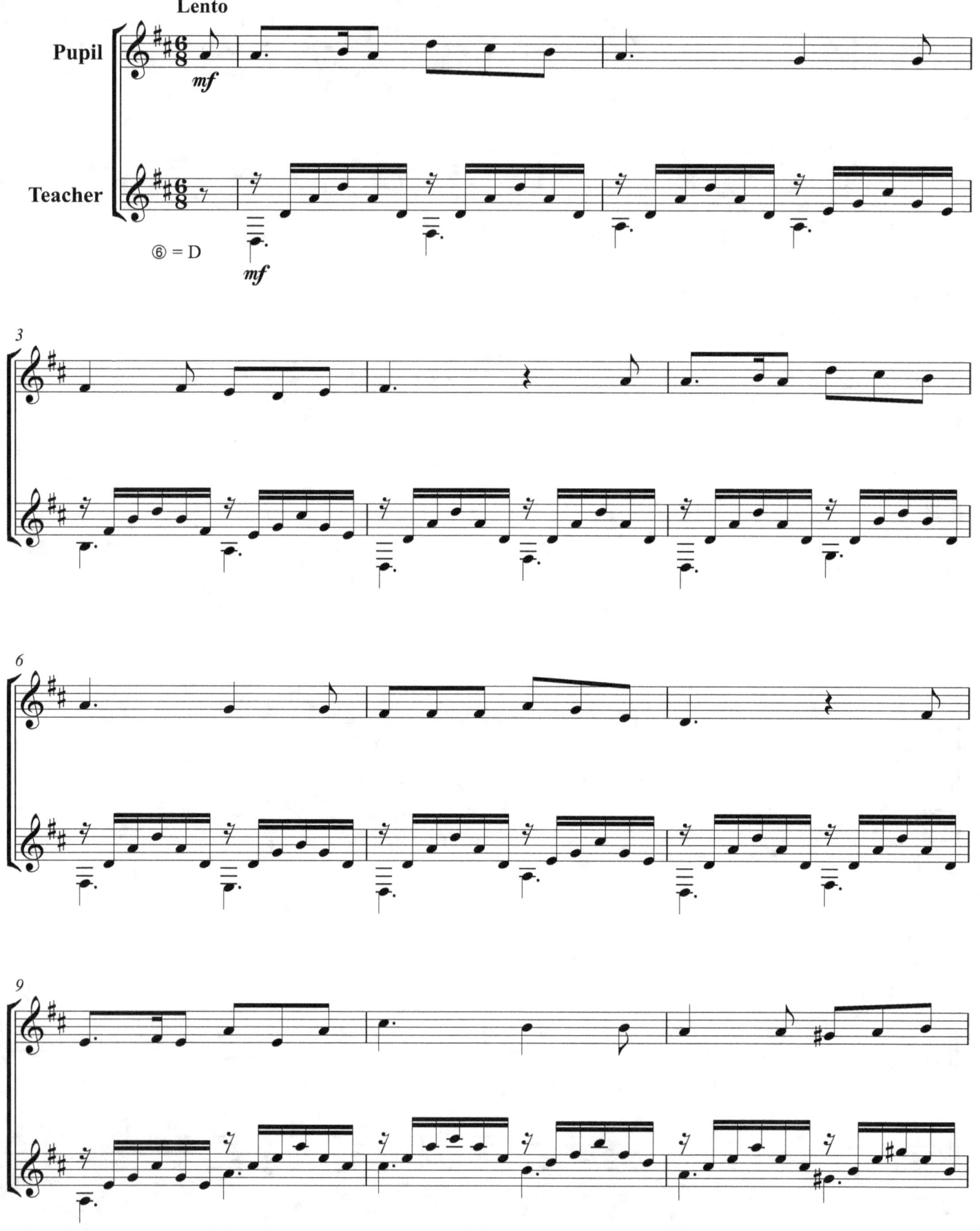

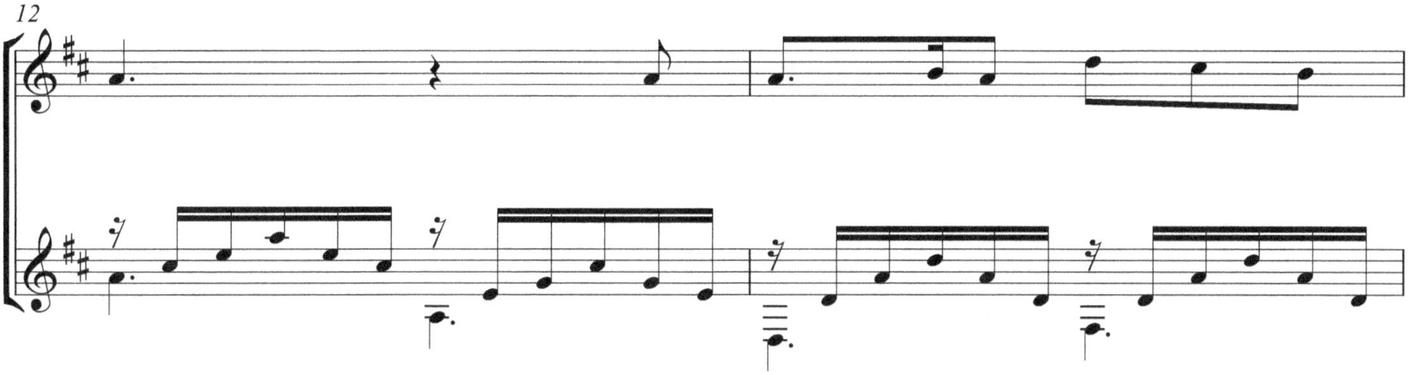

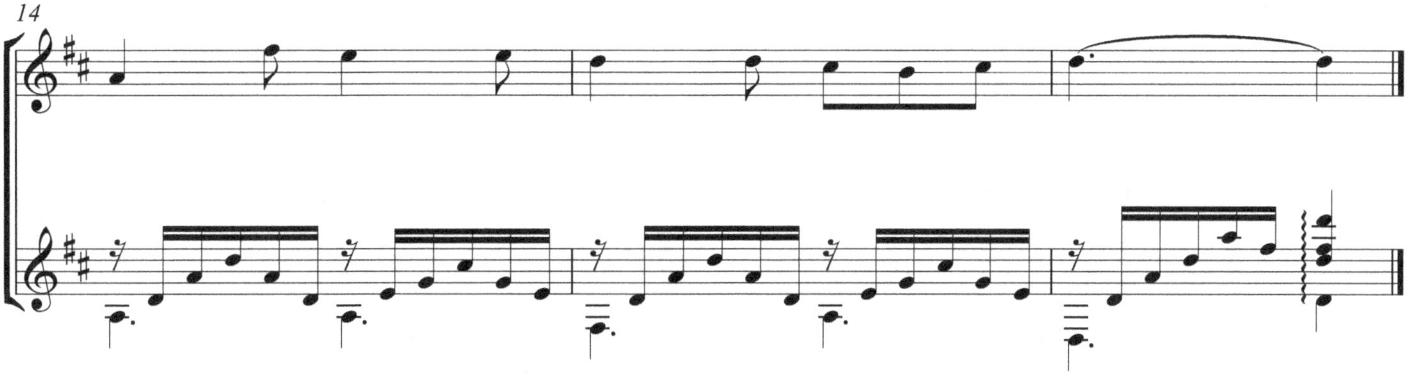

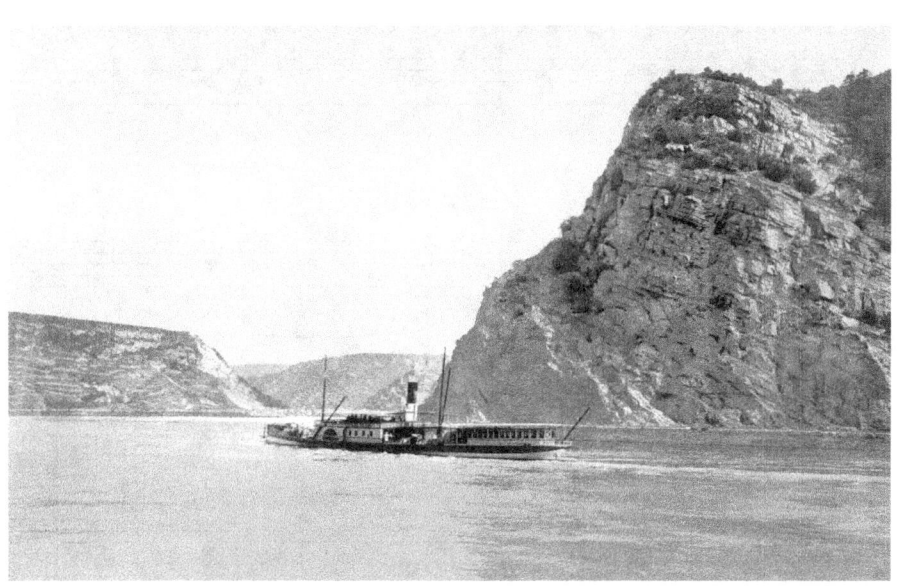

The Lorelei, middle Rhine, Germany

The Life That's Free

Traditional Alsatian

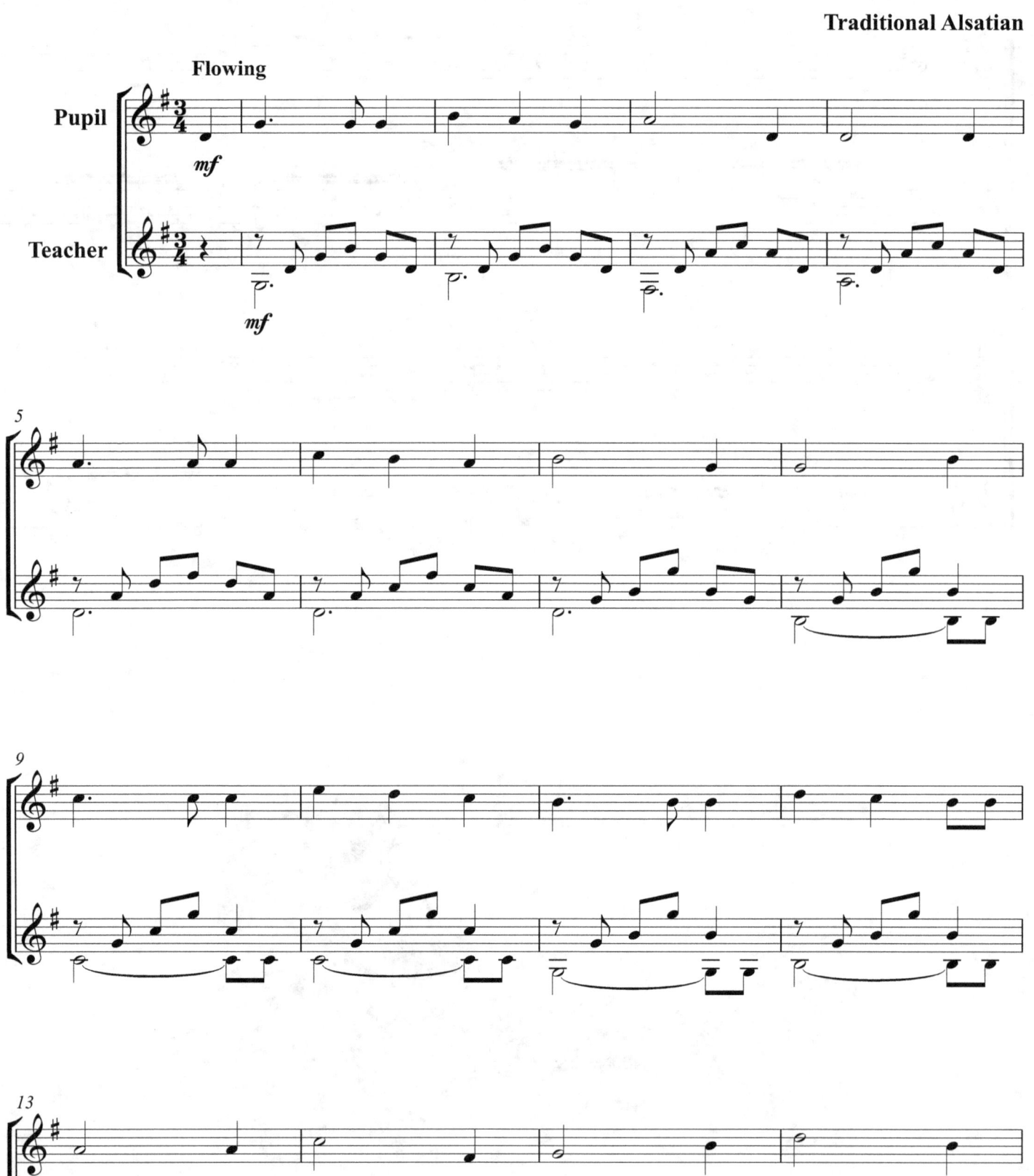

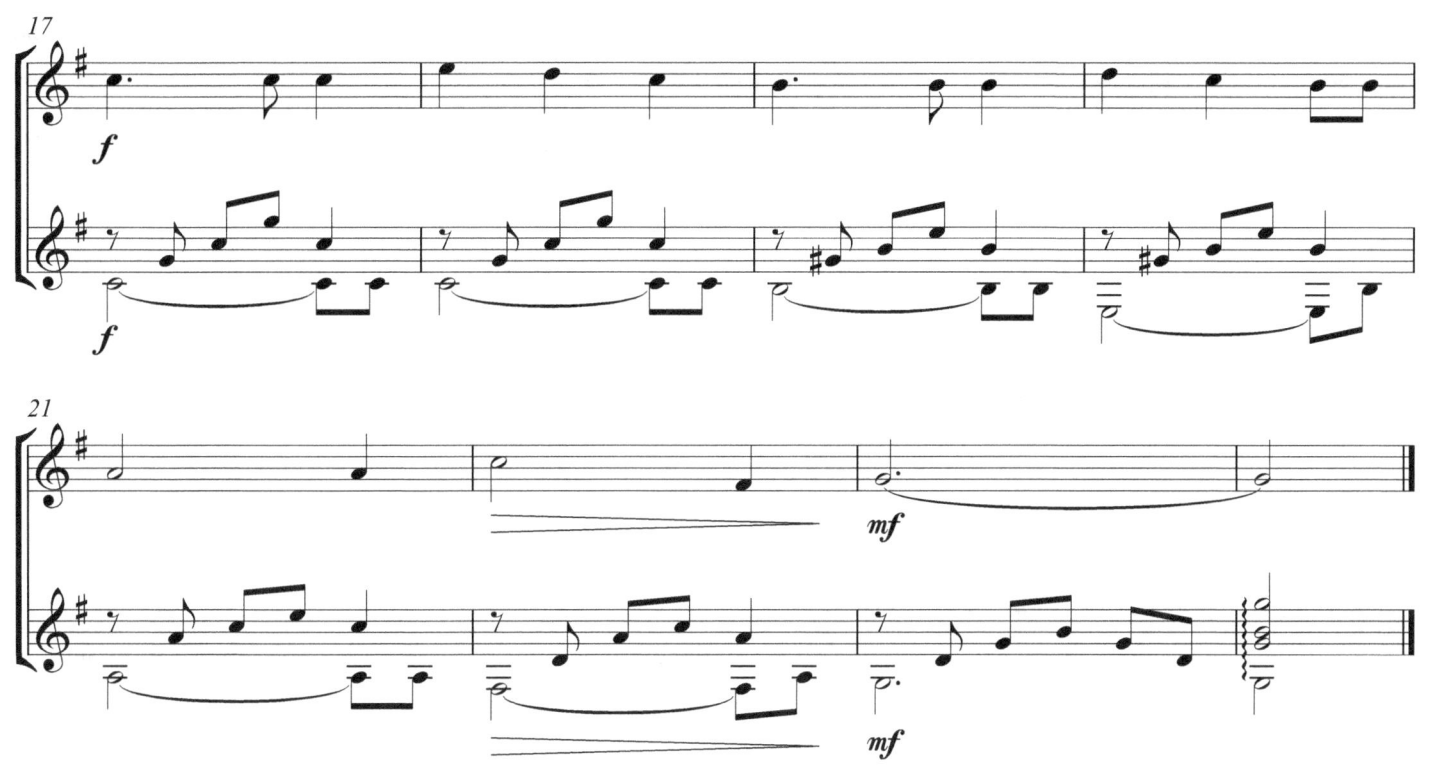

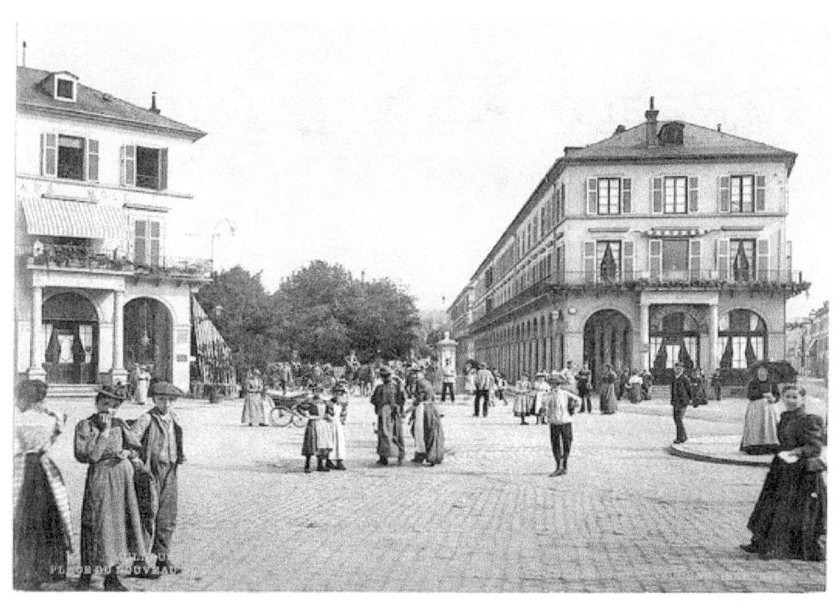

Palace du Quartier Neff MulHausen, Alsace Lorraine

The Minstrel Boy

Traditional Irish

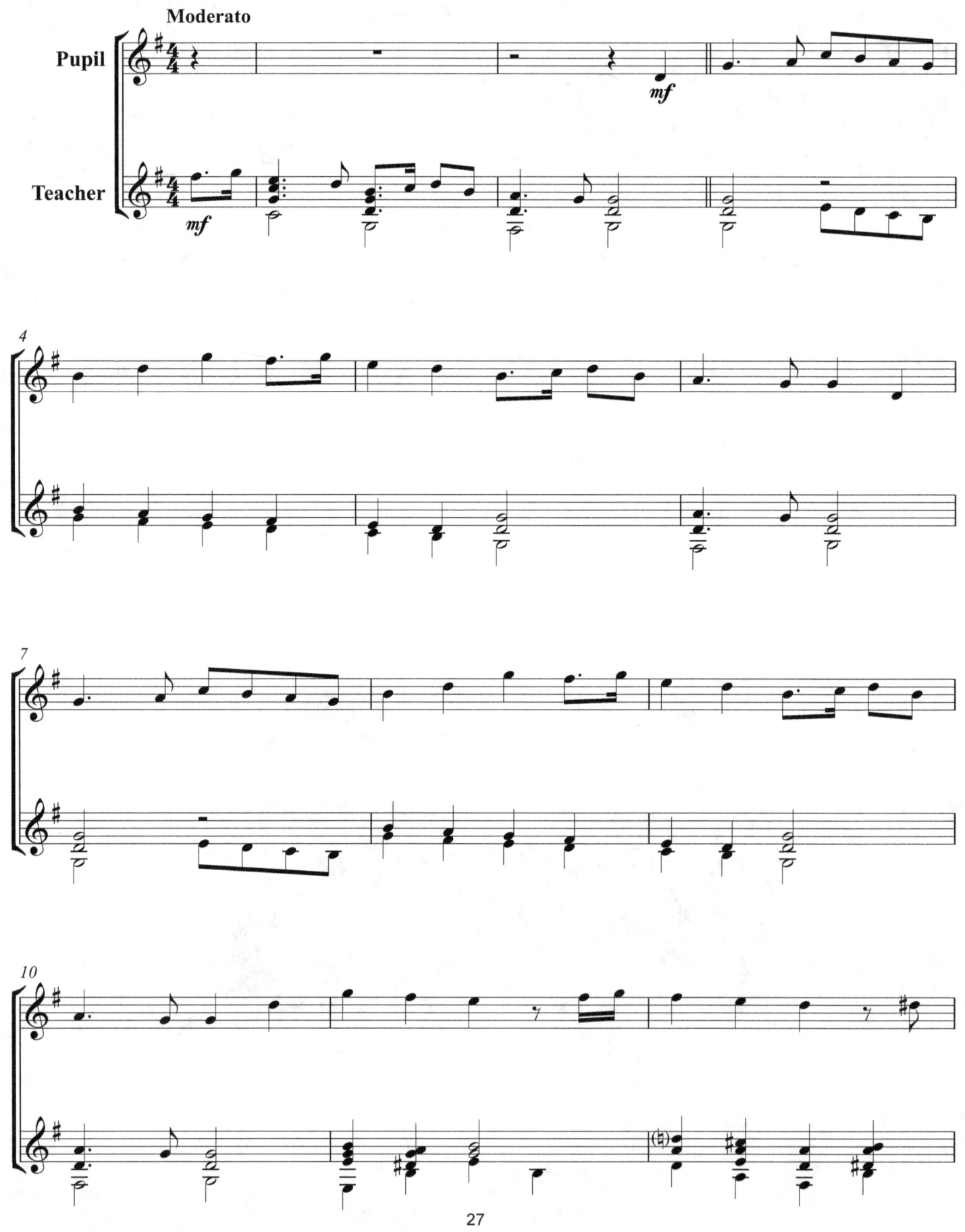

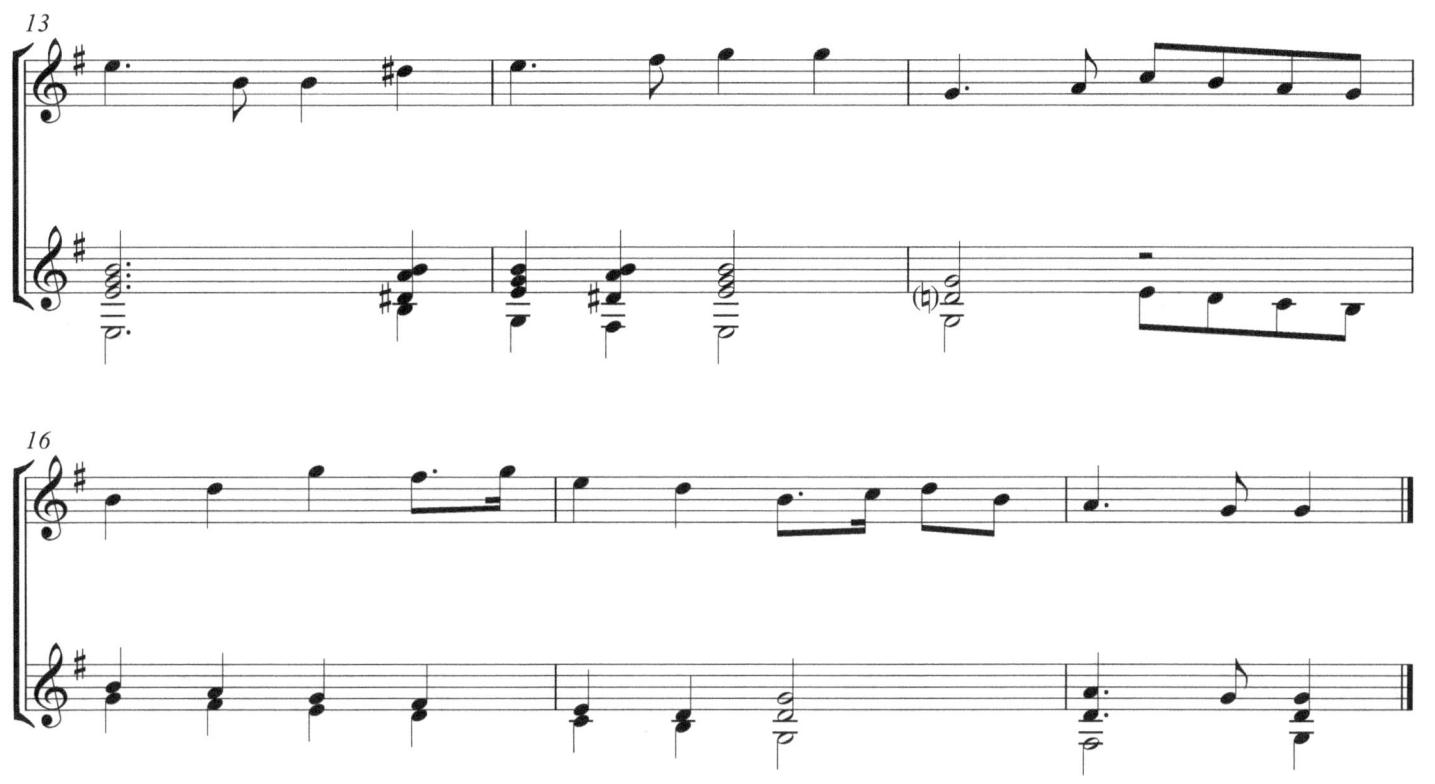

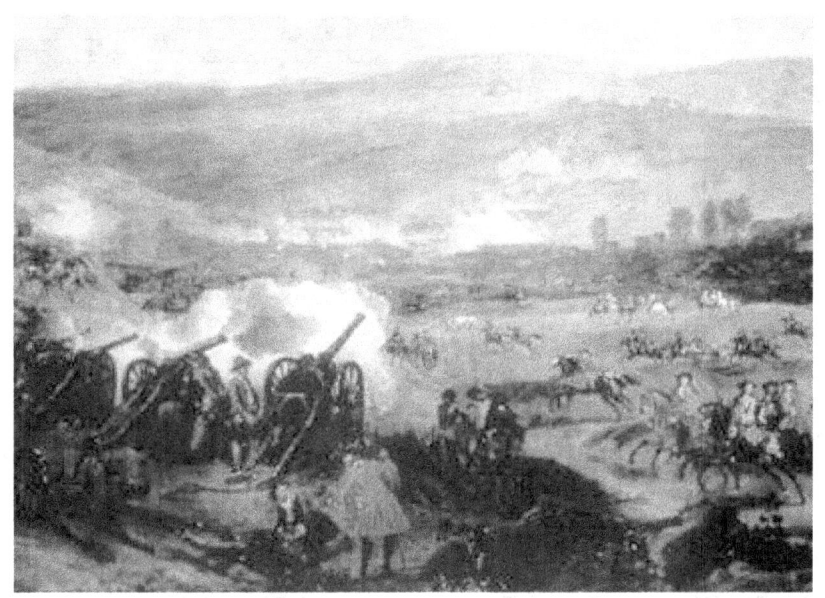

Battle of the Boyne, 1690

Will Ye Go, Lassie

Traditional Irish

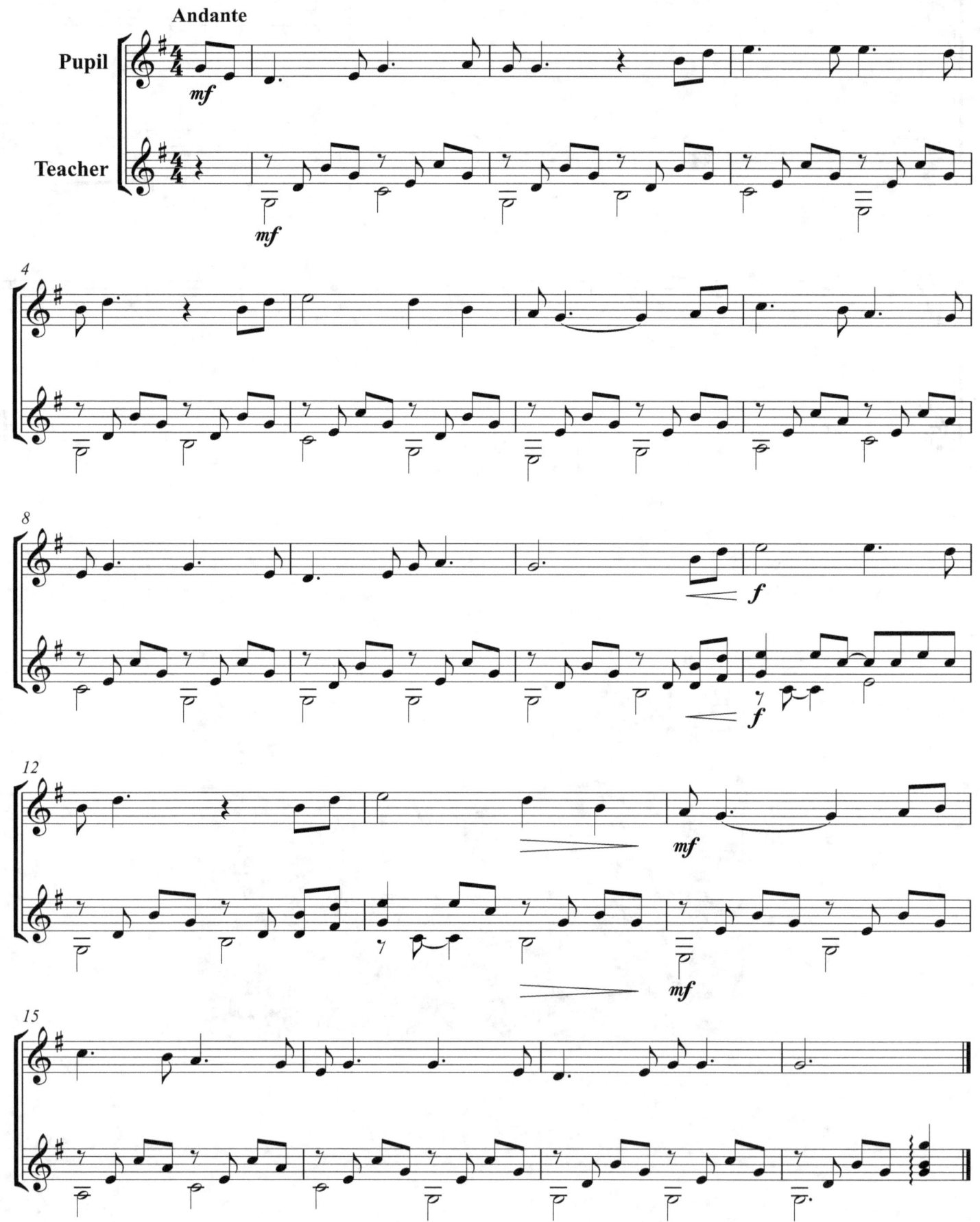

Will Ye No' Come Back Again

Traditional Scottish

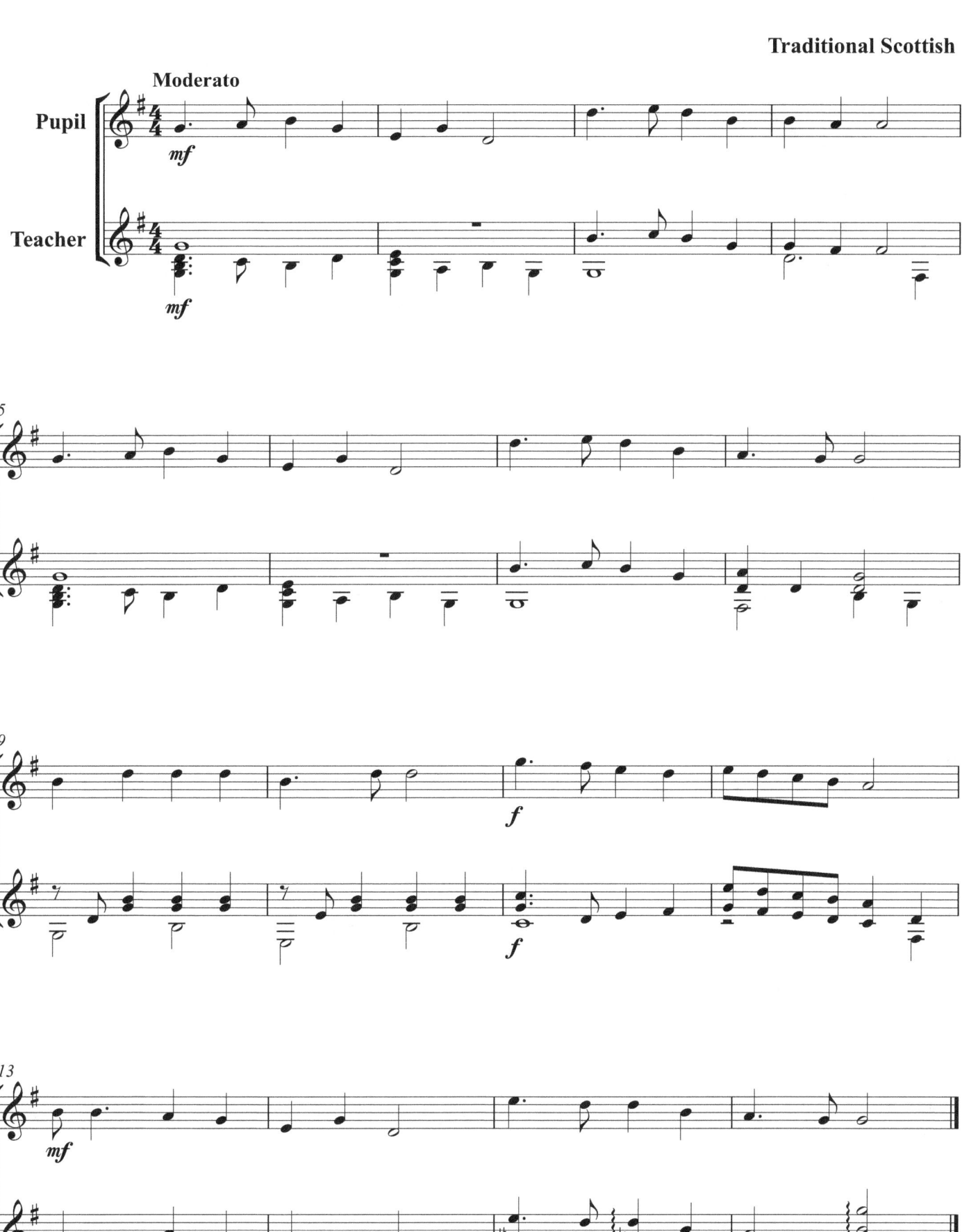

Where The Gentian Blows

Folk Song of Tyrol

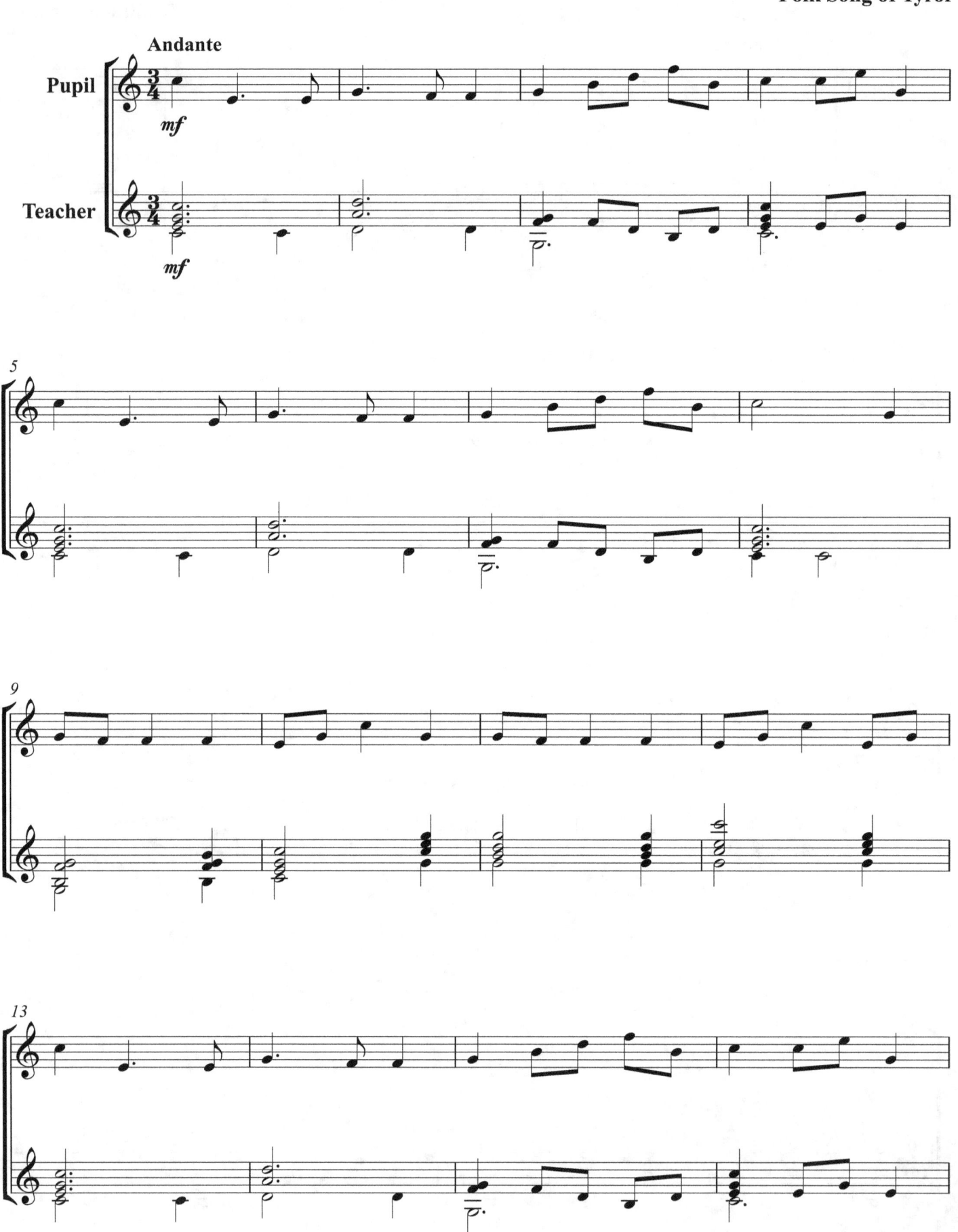

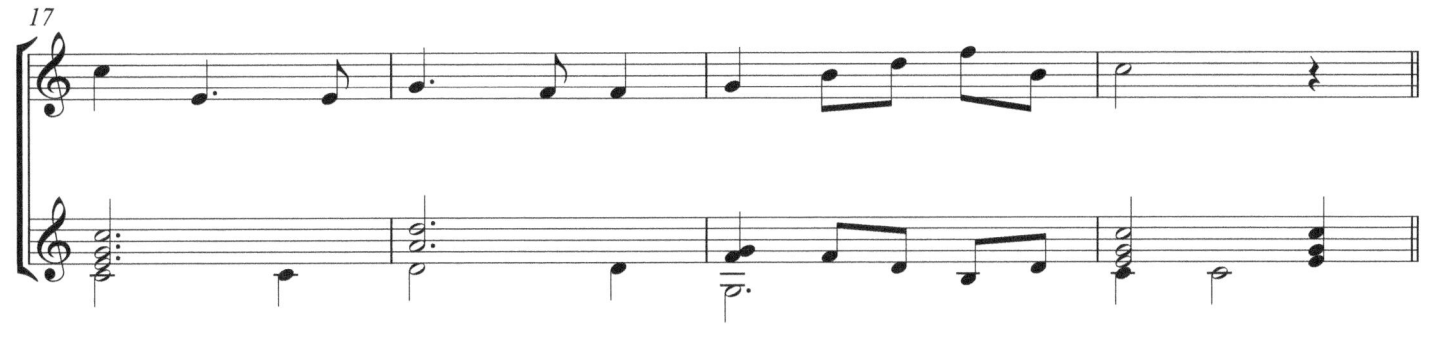

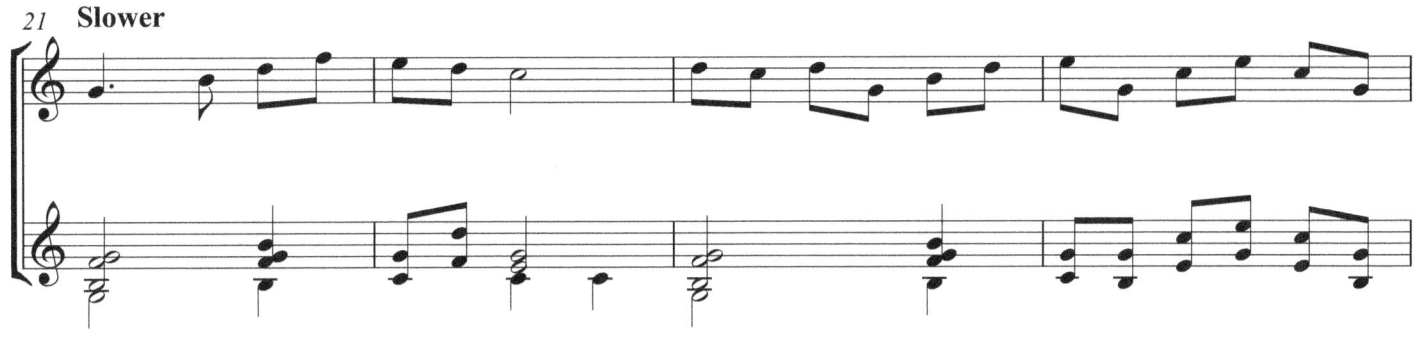

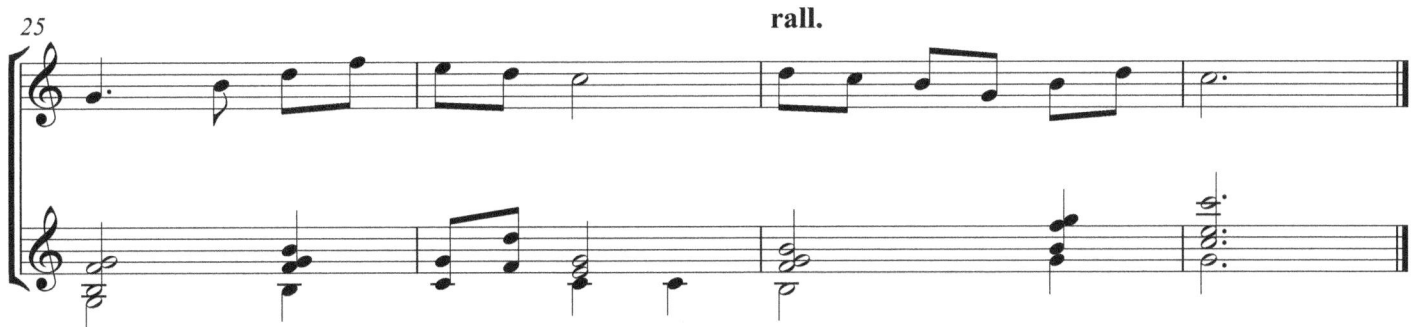

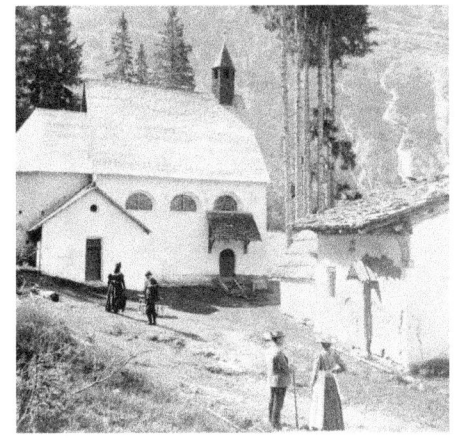

Old Chapel, Tyrol, Austria c. 1899